Praise for *Walk Boldly*

"This book is an essential read for all Black boys and the people who love them."

—**Michael Reid ("Mike the Poet"), author of *Dear Woman***

"*Walk Boldly* is a new favorite for your syllabus, your lectures, and for the young Black men in your life. Through a series of coping strategies and writing prompts, the author brings readers face to face with the negative feelings that stem from every day microaggressions and rejection we know as racism. This is a much-needed guide for the new generations to come."

—**Geoffrey Philp, author of *My Name is Marcus*,
a graphic novel for children**

"*Walk Boldly* teaches our young men to lean into self-love and build a future in which they can be confident and free. This is what I hope to teach my son. That's why he will be reading this book."

—**Matthew Kirby, brainchild and creator of both Honest Human
Resources Consulting LLC and *YNG BLK HR* podcast**

"MJ's *Walk Boldy* is a literary map that will help this and the next generation of Black teen boys to affirm the light within themselves so they may learn to thrive with no brother, son or father left behind."

—**Yanatha Desouvre, writer and filmmaker**

"*Walk Boldly* is the book every young Black man needs to navigate a world filled with systemic racism and survive with their dignity intact. The insights and activities in this book will help you build resilience as you face a world that can be hostile."

—Dr. Emmanuel Cherilien, known as "Dr. Tank," founder and leader of Tank EdDucates, LLC,

"*Walk Boldly* breaks down the challenges Black boys face and gives them tools to deals with them. Along the way, M.J. Fievre teaches Black boys how to be resilient in the face of micro-aggressions and outright racism, without giving into despair."

—Antonio Michael Downing, musician, writer, and activist

"So much talk is given to the notion of resilience, but very few books teach our children how to be resilient. *Walk Boldly* does just that. Every young Black man needs to have a copy of this book in their home library where they can refer to it often."

—Hennessy Williams III, comedian

Walk Boldly

Other books by M.J. Fievre

Black and Resilient:
52 Weeks of Anti-Racist Activities
for Black Joy & Resilience

Resilient Black Girl:
52 Weeks of Anti-Racist Activities
for Black Joy & Resilience

Badass Black Girl:
Quotes, Questions, and Affirmations for Teens

Empowered Black Girl:
Joyful Affirmations and Words of Resilience

Happy, Okay?
Poems about Anxiety, Depression,
Hope and Survival

Raising Confident Black Kids:
A Comprehensive Guide for Empowering Parents
and Teachers of Black Children

Young Trailblazers:
The Book of Black Inventors and Scientists

Young Trailblazers:
The Book of Black Heroes and Groundbreakers

The Book of Awesome Black Women:
Sheroes, Boundary Breakers, and Females who Changed the World

Walk Boldly

Empowerment Toolkit for Young Black Men

By M.J. Fievre

mango
PUBLISHING GROUP

CORAL GABLES

Cover Design & Art Direction: Morgane Leoni
Cover Illustration: berdsigns/Adobe Stock
Layout & Design: Katia Mena

For permission requests, please contact the publisher at:
Mango Publishing Group
2850 S Douglas Road, 4th Floor
Coral Gables, FL 33134 USA
info@mango.bz

For special orders, quantity sales, course adoptions and corporate sales, please email the publisher at sales@mango.bz. For trade and wholesale sales, please contact Ingram Publisher Services at customer.service@ingramcontent.com or +1.800.509.4887.

Walk Boldly: Empowerment Toolkit for Young Black Men

Library of Congress Cataloging-in-Publication number: 2022933237
ISBN: (print) 978-1-64250-733-1, (ebook) 978-1-64250-734-8
BISAC category code YAN051200, YOUNG ADULT NONFICTION / Social Topics / Self-Esteem & Self-Reliance

Printed in the United States of America

Table of Contents

You Are Worthy of a Good, Long, Productive Life

Believing in yourself is key to having a successful future. When you believe in yourself, self-doubt melts away and is replaced by a confidence that will see you through the difficult situations you will face in your life, which can be compounded for a Black boy especially. This book is intended to help you find your belief in yourself and to give you practical advice that will help you achieve your goals. I've included role models for you to look up to and quotes by notable Black leaders that will make you think more about your future and the kind of person you want to become, which ultimately supports the life you end up leading.

I've also included exercises that will help motivate and encourage you to reflect on your current path and how it aligns with the path you desire for your future self and life.

It is easy to become discouraged, and these exercises are here to serve as a reminder of what you can do to make your life better. Ultimately, the "right path" is going to differ by person; the exercises in this book will help you self-reflect and contemplate what that right path is for you—even if it's different than the path the same exercises lead someone else to.

You will need a blank companion journal and pen to be able to reflect and actively complete some of the exercises—so get your materials ready.

〰〰〰

You may wonder: What makes this an essential reading for young Black men?

In one word: Representation.

There is not a lot of positive representation for Black males in mainstream media, which impacts their confidence, self-perception, and may contribute to struggles in identity development or feeling confident within oneself. If society is constantly saying you are one thing and that thing is bad/negative, you need more input within to combat that external narrative. This means that the deposits "we" make in Black males are that much more important, allowing them to subscribe to some things that may be cultural (hair, clothing, shoes, music, etc.) while being able to not define themselves by it completely—and more importantly, not to allow others to define them by it.

Black boys need space to seek and experiment with their identity without it being a death sentence or pre-determination of who they will become later. It's too much pressure and is a confidence killer. There is so much expectation of Black males to assimilate for success and acceptance, so how do they ever get to grow into themselves? As a teacher, my experience with this is advocating for my students and empowering them with information so they can advocate for themselves. Some of my kids love Jordans, want their hair in braids (thanks to the Colin docuseries, they have an ear piercing, and they love Tupac), but they also live in a society where non-Black people mostly appropriate these things, so I teach them how Black people are originators and creators of the culture non-Black people like to play "dress up" in, and that they have to define the line for themselves—who they want to be—and hold that line when up against what others project onto them. Ultimately, I teach them about increased self-awareness to be able to navigate these experiences directly. I also teach them that while it's not their responsibility to do this for others, sometimes in systems of white supremacy and patriarchy, they will have to in order to keep themselves safe.

I understand that teaching you, a Black male, confidence requires:

- Affirming your choices (not policing them)
- Building your self-awareness
- Supporting and encouraging you
- Empowering you with information which arms you to navigate spaces that may not be as accepting
- Providing you with models/mirrors that can inspire and encourage
- Creating spaces for you to understand and differentiate the internal/external as well as your perception of self vs. others' perceptions of you

It isn't easy being a Black boy. There are plenty of stories in the media right now highlighting how little society thinks of young Black men. But you are worthy of a good, long, productive life, and you can make changes to the way other people view Black boys. It all starts by changing how you see yourself and your role in society.

I hope this book will help guide you to a better relationship with yourself and with those around you. It's a small-time investment for a future packed with all good things. You may want to set aside a little time each day to read and practice the exercises in this book. Find a quiet place where you are uninterrupted and can focus on the material in the book.

Keep striving to make your life better!

Kenbe (Be strong!),
M.J. Fievre

WEEKS 1–2: GET A BOOST OF CONFIDENCE

You're living in a world that makes it hard to be Black. You are subject to systemic racism's toll daily, and that can wear on your self-esteem and make your confidence lag. It's important to work actively to undo some of the wear and tear you may feel from other people's expectations, or the limitations placed upon you. Self-confidence is a belief in your abilities to accomplish goals. It means believing in yourself. Confidence is key to having a full life—and you deserve a full life. If you sometimes feel like you just can't believe in yourself anymore, it may be time to get a shot of self-confidence. With a healthy sense of self-confidence, you walk differently through the world. Your stride is more certain and you have a spring in your step. You stand taller. You feel stronger and more able to achieve your goals. Other people's negative opinions and prejudgments matter less, and people are less likely to hassle you because you appear more capable of achieving great things.

Confidence can only come from within, so let's work on our self-worth, our self-care, and our self-awareness this coming week. Nobody is born with loads of self-confidence. It's something we build on every day by being mindful of who we are inside, and who we show to the world. Bring out the best in yourself by nurturing your skills and talents. We all have a unique combination of features and characteristics, an essence that makes us admirable. You may be a math whiz or especially talented artistically. Maybe you're a good listener or have an unusual level of patience. Whatever your talent, it's yours to nurture and develop through practice and learning. And if you're not sure of your talent, you have your whole life to explore and develop your strong suits.

What is certain is that there is no one quite like you on the planet, and you matter. You can make a difference every day, just by showing up and being yourself.

Be you, confidently!

Here are some tips and tricks to take into this week:

1. Stand straight and tall. When you slump, it sends a message to others and to yourself that you have self-doubt. When you get the side-eye at the grocery store from the clerk or the security guard starts asking questions, stand tall. Feel your spine straighten out and put your shoulders back. You have nothing to be ashamed of. You should be proud of who you are, and anyone making a judgment based on a glance isn't considering who you really are individually. Thousands of people have marched and protested to make sure you have the right to walk tall in this world. You were born out of a history of people with inner strength and determination who have done great things, despite being sidelined for the color of their skin. Your people built great libraries in Africa thousands of years ago; they survived slavery and thrived despite it. They have made advances in the modern world. A Black man built the first bloodmobile and invented the first traffic signal. Aside from the history of your people, when you stand tall you feel like you're all that—and you are.

2. Wear something you feel good in this week. You don't have to have the coolest sneakers to feel good about how you look; it's not about having clothes that are a status symbol, so don't feel like you need to spend a lot of money on a wardrobe to feel like a million bucks. When we take the time and effort on our physical appearance this can reflect positively on our thoughts of ourselves. Take the time to groom yourself before you leave your house each day. Look at yourself in the mirror and make sure you're looking fine in your own eyes. Wear your favorite color or your favorite

t-shirt. Take the time to put an effort into your appearance for yourself and not anybody else.

If you feel like you look good, you will send off the vibe that you can take care of yourself—no matter your style. That you're strong and capable—no matter what others think. The truth is, people have lower expectations of you based just on how you look, and the way Black boys present themselves (in hoodies and sneakers etc.) becomes fodder for bias and prejudice. I know many moms and teachers spend time warning their sons and students to pull their pants up or not put a hoodie on because Black boys and young men are often seen by the clothes they wear and judged for how they dress.

But what about feeling good in our culture despite the side-eye we get from others? Black boys have every right to wear what makes them feel good. In fact, in doing so, they often become trend setters, whether it's in the way they wear their hair or their jewelry, or in the way they devote attention to the crispness of a suit or a new pair of Yeezy sneakers. You should take pride in what your people have contributed to the culture on a global scale through aesthetics.

3. Practice your skincare and body care routine every night. Wash your face with warm soapy water and brush your teeth. Take a shower and imagine you're washing off all the stress from the day. This can become a relaxing ritual that will enhance the way you feel in your own skin. It's easy to forget how important a little self-care can be, and Black boys aren't generally encouraged to take care of their bodies. But a strong, clean body will help you have a strong, clear mind. As you grow, pay attention to the features that define you. Maybe your facial hair, or your curls, or your skin require extra attention. Devote the time to those parts of yourself and take

pride in them. The market is brimming with products to help boys and men in their self-care routine—some have even been created by figures you admire on screen and on sports fields. Self-care is important. When you feel good about yourself, others feel good about you, and your confidence is boosted.

4. Know that you are unique and own it. If you aren't sure of who you are exactly, take the time to explore the different aspects of yourself and try out new things. Don't fall into the trap of comparing yourself to other people. You are uniquely you. It can be hard when everyone on social media is getting attention and likes and you are not, but you do you.

5. Social media gives us a false image of what's going on; people are posting things they want you to see, and you're not getting the whole picture. We all carry around self-doubts and insecurities, and those don't necessarily show up on Instagram feeds. It's easy to become a jealous, spiteful person when you spend too much time comparing yourself to others instead of building yourself up.

    Social media is a breeding ground for such behavior. In fact, the National Center for Health Research found that 45 percent of adolescents reported being online "almost constantly," and another 44 percent reported being online "at least several times a day." Most concerning about that study was the findings on these teens' mental health as a result to social media exposure. The study continues to note that "although social media can allow people to reach out and connect with others, it can also make some people feel worse. Almost 25 percent of adolescents believe that social media has a mostly negative effect... ."[1]

---

1   https://www.center4research.org/social-media-affects-mental-health/

The specific problem addressed here has to do with the constant comparison to others, or that feeling young people experience regarding their self-image. Social media projects the false notion that there is an ideal for the body, and that those who consume those images should strive to be just as perfect. "Higher social media use leads to 'body surveillance,' which refers to monitoring one's own body and becoming judgmental of it. People who do more body surveillance report feeling more shame about their bodies. Looking at profiles of attractive people leads to more negative body image. There are many 'fitspiration' accounts on Instagram, posting about diet and exercise in order to be thin, and it is common for people to filter or photoshop their posts on Instagram in order to remove blemishes. People compare themselves to these ideals or these edited images and feel like they do not measure up. This can cause poor body image."

If you find that you're comparing yourself to other people, take a minute to ask yourself what you've done lately to deserve recognition. Have you studied as hard as you could in school? Have you been spending enough time with your family? Are you in regular contact with your friends? Have you been focusing on meeting your goals? Focusing on your own self-worth and how you spend your time will give you a better sense of self. Let other people be who they are. If you are focused on your own growth, you can be happy for your friends when they have news to be proud of. Make yourself the most important person in your life, and other people will take notice of you. This doesn't mean you stop caring about other people, but try putting your own needs and goals first.

6. Practice what you're good at doing. Sometimes acknowledging our talents leads to greater confidence in ourselves. You know what you have to offer the world in different situations and can move through the world

with self-assurance. Let's say you're talented at building, engineering, mechanics, or something more artistic like painting or arranging music. Spend as much time as you can developing that talent. Go to architecture centers, engineering workshops, visit museums or music studios, and look at work by other artists. Really study the craft behind your talent, so you know how it works. And celebrate little victories. You don't have to throw a party, but at least give yourself a pat on the back when you're successful at something that you worked really hard on. Take a moment to acknowledge to yourself that you've done something to be proud of. Tell yourself, "Well done!" and allow yourself a moment to take pride in your achievement by feeling it in your body.

7. Show kindness to others. Doing good for others helps lift us up. In turn, we feel more confident. There are lots of ways to be kind to others. If you see someone having a rough day, ask them if they need anything. Sometimes they may just need you to hear them vent their frustrations. If you see someone struggling, help them out. Hold the door for the delivery man wheeling boxes into a business, for example. Or help the lady who's juggling too many grocery bags. If you look closely at the world around you, you'll notice when people need help. And it's a two-way street: Build meaningful relationships with people who think highly of you and are kind to you. Having a support system of close friends is important. It keeps you from becoming lonely and isolated and can boost your self-confidence. When you're having a bad day, there's nothing like having a friend just sit and listen to you and tell you everything will be okay. Find people who are willing to be there when you need them. It can be hard to show people you're having a hard time, so

find people you can trust, and don't be afraid to lean on them for support. We all need a friend from time to time. The best way to do this is by being there for someone who needs you to let them know it's going to be okay.

8. Know and understand your core values. Core values are the things in life that are very important and central to your personality. For example, maybe you think honesty is very important. That's a core value. Believing that honesty is very important means you have a hard time telling a lie. Understanding who you are fully as you evolve and grow brings great self-assurance. It might help you to make a list of your core values. Do you believe in hard work? Do you believe in determination? What do you really believe is important in life? Ask yourself that and build a list you can grow as you mature.

SPOTLIGHT ON A BLACK ROLE MODEL

"As a child, I knew that people had a certain expectation of what a reader (or scholar) should look like, and I was well aware that I didn't fit that expectation. But my mother encouraged me to think of myself differently. She'd also tell others about me: 'I bet he can outscore you on any test.' "

—**Akili Nzuri**, writer, educator, literary influencer, curator of www.ablackmanreading.com

INTROSPECTION:

Understanding Self-Confidence

This first exercise is a three-part exercise that will get you thinking about the difference between being self-confident and having self-doubts.

To start, think of a situation where you felt self-confident, and it made a difference in how you approached the situation.

Then, ask yourself the following questions:

- What was the situation you found yourself in? What was happening that required you to rely on your self-confidence?
- How did you speak to yourself in this situation? What kind of self-talk did you use?
- How did you feel physically? Where did you feel different sensations in your body? What were these sensations?
- How did you handle the situation? What did you do to resolve the experience?

Next, think of a situation where you were filled with self-doubts and answer the same four questions.

Lastly answer the following three questions:

- What can I say to myself when I feel doubtful that will bring me self-confidence?
- What can I do in a situation that will bring me self-confidence? An example of something you could do is to create an affirmation that will boost your feelings of self-worth.
- The next time I'm in a similar situation, what can I do differently to change how things worked out?

WEEKS 3–4: KNOW YOUR OWN SELF-WORTH

Black male youth receive so much information about who they are and who they will become from a myriad of sources. The media paints its own narrative. Parents—parenting from fear, safety, their own personal experiences, history, etc.—push their own narrative and agenda. Peers, music, TV, movies, etc. push a variety of agendas. There are so many conflicting messages, expectations, warnings, and projections. What is necessary is that Black male youth feel empowered to define themselves and to find value in how they define themselves—even if it goes against the myriad of sources. Black male youth are more than stereotypes, rap music, violence, drugs, alcohol, sex, gangs, sports, dying young—but they're also more than assimilation and watering themselves down to fit it. They're sons, cousins, brothers, nephews, friends, students, future husbands, future fathers, etc. These roles help add to their self-worth because they construct meaning around identity, but in addition to that, it's important that Black boys explore the possibilities of who they are in the present and may want to become in the future—worth is supported by assessing and developing your values, strengths, interests, passions, abilities, contributions, etc. so to develop self-worth, they need to spend time doing things that will align accordingly.

Having a positive or negative view on our self-worth affects many things throughout life. If you don't value yourself, chances are no one else will either. It's easier to achieve your goals and stand up for yourself if you believe you are worth it. It will greatly change the way you choose to react to certain situations. Knowing you are of value will make it easier for you when you must face racism in your life or when someone dismisses you because of the color of your skin. It will affect how you treat yourself and others. When you value yourself, you're kinder. You take better care of yourself and are nicer to other people. You know that other people's criticisms of you are just their opinions. Besides, you're stuck with yourself for the rest of your life. Why would you want to spend time with someone you have a low opinion of? Be your own best friend instead.

1. Give yourself more credit and trust yourself. Of course, you can! Set goals that stretch your limits and work hard to achieve them. Let's say you're in high school and you're having a hard time in your Spanish class. You're barely pulling a C. Set the goal of bringing your grade up to a B, and then study your Spanish to meet your goal. Once you've earned a B, try for an A the next semester. You can do it. Focus on your own skills and talents when feeling inadequate. We all have our strong suits and should appreciate our own accomplishments. Let us also take the time to nourish and refine our own set of talents. When we work on what we are good at, we will begin to feel better about ourselves. Think of all that you have accomplished with your hard work and perseverance. We all deserve to be proud of our own accomplishments. Sometimes it is hard to see how far we have come until we look back on the journey.

2. Learn what others appreciate about you. Ask them. We often do not view ourselves in the same light as our friends and family. Our loved ones will see the talent, skills, and positive attributes we do not see. Hearing from those close to us that we are awesome and badass can knock some sense into us. Remove the influences in your life that do not make you feel good about yourself. Social media can be a big one since it can be a highlight reel for many people. For example, if you follow someone who makes you feel negatively about yourself when you see their posts, unfollow them. You want to fill your life with things that inspire you, not things that promote negative emotions.

3. Stop comparing. When we compare ourselves to others, we run the risk of ruining our chances at happiness. Suddenly, we get tied up in where we are lacking instead of focusing on what we have going for us right now and our unique qualities. Each of us has unique strengths and talents that make us individuals. Instead, try celebrating your uniqueness and focus on appreciating yourself. Take your negative feelings and turn them into a positive outcome. Don't compare yourself to others. It's a waste of energy; it weighs you down. Focus on your goals, and you'll be amazed at how much more driven you are when you take others out of the equation. Do not try to live your life aiming to beat out everyone around you. You will only become disappointed and negative. Life is not a competition. You are the only person who can change how you see the world.

4. Make time for yourself and use the time for self-reflection. Spend some time alone with yourself doing what makes you happy, whether it's taking a walk, shooting hoops, or relaxing with a good movie and a snack. Take a little quiet time at the end of each day to reflect and think about what went well for you. Without time for ourselves, we can lose track of our own wants and needs. We all need time to recharge so we can face the next day or tackle the next project.

SPOTLIGHT ON A BLACK ROLE MODEL

To develop your self-worth, it's important not to be a follower but to be a leader. **Oluwatoyin Ayanfodun**, founder of Tomorrow's Leaders NYC, gives some advice for anyone who sometimes feels they conform to the opinions of others:

"Don't let the opinion of someone else automatically become your own."

The Self-Worth Fuel Tank

This exercise will feel a bit familiar, reminding you of Week 2, about getting a boost of confidence. This might be because self-confidence and self-worth are all more similar than different. You may ask: How can these two be differentiated? I suggest you think of self-worth as an internal perception of self, how much value you put on yourself. Self-confidence on the other hand is internal mindset paired with external behavior.

This exercise is designed to refill your Self-Worth Fuel Tank. It highlights the accomplishments, events, moments, thoughts, and feelings that contribute to having a full "self-worth tank," that works as a source of motivation and replenishment for when it's difficult and you need reassurance to move forward confidently.

You'll want ten to fifteen minutes of free time to accomplish it. Start by dividing a sheet of paper into three columns labeled ACCOMPLISHMENT OR MOMENT, THOUGHTS AND FEELINGS, and SIGNIFICANCE. In the first column, think back on things you've accomplished over the past month, six months, and then years—or moments/events that filled you with confidence. Write them down quickly. In the second column, write down the feelings and thoughts associated with each entry. In the third column write down why each accomplishment or moment was significant to you. You many even include a goal you have that will grow and further extend that accomplishment to the next level.

WEEKS 5–6:
CREATE BALANCE, OVERCOME BURNOUT, AND ELIMINATE ROADBLOCKS

Being Black (in America especially and in oppressive societies overall) is exhausting. Furthermore, being a teenager is also exhausting. When it comes to being Black in an oppressive society that specifically oppresses people of color, you are constantly bombarded with traumatic images, news updates, events, etc. There's trauma on every corner. Every other week, an unarmed Black person is killed (often male), a Black person is unfairly sentenced for a crime in comparison to their non-Black counterparts, and negative stereotypical outcomes are constantly highlighted above the positive ones. These experiences are exhaustive and daunting and must be balanced with the alternative. The inverse. The positive things that happen with just as much frequency but not enough amplification due to marginalization. This is the balance Black youth need to learn. Yes, be informed, but be cautious about biases that prevail and about agendas. Also, seek out the alternative, even if mainstream isn't pushing it. It's there. Surround yourself with it. Use it as a buffer/filter. For every negative deposit made by the media, Black boys may experience a withdrawal, so it's important they have positive deposits to offset their internal balances.

When it comes to being a teen, it can feel like constantly being misunderstood.

Balance is key to preventing burnout. Burnout generally means you care a lot about what you're doing; you've just hit a brick wall because you've spent too much energy on the same task. Parental demands, societal demands, pressure to succeed and have things figured out, navigating relationships—all with a still-developing pre-frontal cortex, peer pressure, and hormonal fluctuations. These can all lend themselves to burnout. As educator Oluwatoyin Ayanfodun, founder of Tomorrow's Leaders NYC, explained to us during an interview, peer pressure is the most important cause of burnout. Peer pressure comes in many forms, both verbal and nonverbal. You worry about what your parents expect from you. At the same time, you want to fit in, to be liked, to stand out. For some of you, there's the pressure to join gangs, to get into fights, to disconnect from school.

Expecting too much from ourselves mentally and physically or taking on too much work can lead to lack of motivation. We burn up all our energy quickly instead of using it wisely. It can be tricky to find the right balance between working hard and working yourself to exhaustion.

Use these tips to learn and practice prevention from burnout:

1. Learn to prioritize. Make lists of things you need to do in order of importance. This means knowing what's most important and understanding that some tasks are not as important. If you have a prioritized list, you can check off the most important things on it first, and then work your way through the less important tasks. You can tell which tasks are most important by knowing when they are due, how much work you'll need to put into each task, and whether you need to accomplish one task before moving on to the next step.

   Time management is an important skill to develop to get your tasks done on time. It also helps prevent feelings of becoming overwhelmed. If you can organize your day in a way that makes sense to you, you'll see a big difference.

   At the beginning of each week, write a list of the things you need to accomplish in the upcoming week. Just the act of writing it down is useful. You'll be more likely to remember what tasks you must accomplish, and you'll be less likely to forget items on your list.

Take your weekly task list and break it down into daily lists of things you need to do each day. You'll feel less anxious if you break your big goals down into manageable tasks. That way you can see progress as you complete each step toward your goal.

2. Set personal and professional boundaries. Learn how to say no when needed. It is never a bad thing to protect your peace. Having healthy boundaries means letting people know what you are willing to take on. You can't expect the other person to know your limits unless you communicate them clearly. Often, we're afraid to set boundaries because we fear the other person will think we're making a judgment on them. Think of it this way: If someone is standing on your foot, you'd tell them. It wouldn't mean they were a bad person, it would just mean you need them to get off your foot.

3. Speak up. If you are feeling overwhelmed, let someone know. Young boys and young men are often taught to be tough to the point where they can't ask for help, which often leaves them feeling burdened with the task of problem-solving and taking care of everything themselves. As a result, they sometimes take on too much. It's okay to get overwhelmed. We all do. But to be successful, other people need to know when you're struggling so you can take a break or get some help. It's perfectly okay to ask for help.

4. Take breaks throughout the day when needed. If you find it hard to stay focused or if your mind begins to wander, make sure to take a breather. If you overwork yourself, it can

lead you to put things off or to burnout. You have enough stress on you already, and keep in mind, you may have to work harder than your peers for less recognition. It can be difficult to find the right balance when the world wants you to go, go, go. Rest allows our bodies and minds to function at their best. If you become overworked, you'll have a harder time making the most of your productive time.

Do some quick stretches, close your eyes, and rejuvenate yourself by drinking water or taking a walk to get some fresh air. Take a break from your current task, and work on a different task for a little while to re-engage your focus. Often, you'll find that the motivation is waiting for you when you get back to the task you had to put to the side for a while.

5. Get away to reset and recharge. We all need a change of scenery at times to find new inspiration or to collect our thoughts and nurture our energy. If you can't plan a vacation, take a couple days off to relax close to home. Plan some time in nature near where you live. Go to the park, hop in your kayak, find new trails to hike. Spending time outdoors is a sure way to reconnect with the real world and feel more grounded, and sunshine, especially for those who can afford it, helps to recharge batteries.

6. Accept that sometimes unexpected events come up. You can plan your day down to the minute, but life has a way of throwing unwanted surprises at you, good or bad. Be prepared for the unexpected. Plan free time in your day to make up for the surprise events that come along. If you have extra time allotted, you'll be more likely to have the time to get through everything on your to do list.

7. Embrace imperfection. As much as we'd all like to be perfect, it's just not possible. Accept that you will make mistakes and learn from them when you do. You're always learning. Think of a baby when it's learning to walk. It has to fall down a lot before it's sure on its feet. It's the same with most of the things we learn. Mastering a new skill takes patience and practice. As you grow, things that are hard right now will get easier.

Failure is not the enemy. Once we try something and fail, we often feel like quitting. Don't fall into this trap. We grow and become better by failing. Instead, don't allow yourself to linger on negative emotions. Focus instead on the lessons you learned and do better once you try again. Remember the F.A.I.L. acronym: First Attempt In Learning. If you can remember that learning is a process, it makes it easier to see failure as just another step in learning.

"There should be a level of balance between the professional and personal. I have two daughters and they force balance in me because their success is paramount, more important even than the work I do at Hello Tractor. I prioritize their needs, which forces me to have some level of balance. For example, my workday today was broken up by me taking my daughter to her gymnastics class. Balance is built into my schedule to some degree. And then other aspects of my day-to-day force me to be more intentional. My wife and I have to find time for each other and set boundaries because we work in similar professions. We both work in tech and in agriculture. So it's easy to be consumed by professional talk. We have to set up boundaries there as well. Certainly you have to be intentional."

—Jehiel Oliver, entrepreneur

INTROSPECTION:

Create and Maintain Personal Boundaries

Setting boundaries can be difficult if you aren't used to asserting yourself. But the more you practice setting boundaries, the easier it becomes. To set a boundary, state clearly what you want or don't want using non-emotional language like, "I won't be going to the gathering tonight." Practice saying no and sticking to it. Safeguard your personal spaces. Only allow people in that you trust. Find a group of supportive friends and family who will help back you up when you are setting boundaries. Along with setting boundaries, asking for what you want can be challenging. Try asking one person for one thing today. Be clear in what you want: "I want fifteen minutes of uninterrupted time to myself." When you state your desires, you'll see pretty quickly that people will try to accommodate you if they can.

Some sentences that demonstrate assertiveness are:

- "No."
- "Thanks, but I can't make that a priority right now."
- "Thanks for thinking of me, but I think I'll pass on this one."

WEEKS 7–8:
BUILD A GROWTH
MINDSET

These days, the term "growth mindset" flows easily in conversation. Motivational speakers tell us about using growth mindset as we move forward to achieve our goals, and influencers are using technology to amplify the idea of growth mindset. We are consuming praises for this concept from all mediums, but what does growth mindset really mean?

To understand the true meaning of a growth mindset, you must also consider its opposite: fixed mindset.

A fixed mindset applies to those who believe that if they are not naturally gifted with a talent for something, they will never be good at it. Any attempt at learning to become good at it would be a waste of time for a person with a fixed mindset. They don't believe they ever can.

A growth mindset on the other hand applies to those who believe that natural talent is not enough, that one must continuously work hard to achieve their goals. People with a growth mindset are not afraid to learn new things and they don't allow their growth or potential to be limited.

Stanford Professor and Psychologist Dr. Carol Dweck noted that students with growth mindsets "see 'confronting challenges, profiting from mistakes, and persevering in the face of setbacks,' as ways to become smarter, and that it is within their control to achieve higher levels of performance."[2]

Growth mindset for Black people in general can sometimes feel misleading because it's impossible to utilize growth mindset to overcome system racism and oppression. However, growth

---

2 https://www.amle.org/grit-and-growth-mindset-deficit-thinking/

mindset can be utilized to propel oneself and one's community efforts forward within reasonable expectations and realistically thinking; while it may not "fix" the things outside of your control, it does have a positive impact on endurance and perseverance that I think is beneficial, all things considered. There's a social-emotional intelligence to being able to differentiate how it can work for us as people of color living within systems not necessarily designed for us or by us. As my editor, Nathaniel Parker, explained to me, "A growth mindset allows you to believe in the talents that you do possess, and to identify those skills you still need to develop. With a growth mindset, you show an openness to sharpening those skills. You never think that you're at the peak—you strive for better."

Our lives are full of daily challenges and experiences we learn from as we grow. Having a growth mindset means you are looking to grow your experiences and skill set. You don't want to be stuck in the same rut you've been in for a while now. It also means you look for opportunities to grow and expand your mind. Try to stay open to what the world has to offer you and build the joy in your life. Building anything takes time and thoughtfulness, so be patient with yourself. Start this week building a growth mindset and see how far you go.

1. Be open to learning something new from the unexpected. Unexpected events are just a part of life. It's what you take away from the experience in terms of lessons that matters most. Let go of fear or anger when something unexpected happens and instead, examine what happened and try to learn from it.

2. Acknowledge your own faults and learn what you can change. Maybe you're impatient. Patience is something you can learn through practice. When we recognize our own faults, we can find ways to better handle them to achieve happiness. No one is perfect, and it's important not to let perceived flaws stunt progress. Learn from criticism. Receiving a critique does not have to be completely negative. First, ask yourself if the opinion holds value for you. Then, think of how you can improve next time. Learning to receive criticism sends a message that you respect the person giving you advice. Criticism is not necessarily a judgment on you. It could just be that someone else sees things differently and is offering you another viewpoint.

3. Learn to enjoy the process. A lesson learned may not always be pleasant but focusing on the good can help. Sometimes when it feels like you're not getting anywhere, you are close to a breakthrough. Other times it means you're just progressing at a slower pace than what you expect. Don't rush. When we expect something too quickly or rush the process, we are often left disappointed. Take small steps toward your goals and you'll get there.

4. Don't stop motivating yourself when you accomplish a goal. Always continue to build on your success if it adds to your overall happiness. If you pulled your grade up to a B, try for an A. If you ran a mile in ten minutes, see if you can run even faster.

5. Don't shy away from challenges. Look at them as opportunities for growth. Something that seems impossible at first will be easier to achieve if you break it down into manageable steps and tackle it one step at a time.

6. Pay attention to what you think and say. If your words are negative and dark, your mindset will be, too. Try to remain positive. Tell yourself you're getting there, even if it feels like you're moving backward. When you are positive, you're more likely to grow. This will be discussed at length in Weeks 9–10, and 11–12 when we discuss negative thoughts and how to overcome them.

7. Learn from the mistakes of others. If you can see where other people go wrong, you can avoid making the same kinds of mistakes.

SPOTLIGHT ON A BLACK ROLE MODEL

"A growth mindset allows you to go after your dreams and be the best that you can be. It pushes you to challenge yourself no matter what room or what environment you're in, whether you're in college, whether you're building a company, whether you're working with Microsoft or WeWork, which I've been grateful enough to do. I've always wanted to challenge myself to see what else I can do and what else I can achieve."

—**Tim Salau**, Mr. Future of Work, CEO of Guide, Global Tech Influencer

INTROSPECTION:

Take on an Alter Ego

Jesse Owens said, "The battles that count aren't the ones for gold medals. The struggles within yourself—the invisible, inevitable battles inside all of us—that's where it's at." The next time you're feeling down, try out an alter ego. Pick a personality you can emulate and pretend to be someone else. Ask yourself: What would this alter ego do? What would they say? Adopting an alter ego can support a growth mindset. When you are developing a skill for yourself, sometimes adopting the persona of someone who has developed that same skill very well can be a confidence booster and encouragement to you as you work to grow the skill in yourself. In fact, this idea echoes our previous discussion in Week One, about standing straight and tall in the shadow of those who came before you. Your ancestors were also men and women with skills. If you can be inspired by them, these same ancestors can guide you into adopting the right alter ego to get you where you hope to go.

WEEKS 9–10: PRACTICE OPTIMISM AND FIND THOSE SILVER LININGS

No matter how many times you've been told to be an optimist, your whole life you probably had a vague idea of what that meant. Looking at things differently, in a new light, and hoping for the best outcomes are traits of optimism. Ad yet, as it is with the growth mindset, Black America finds itself constantly riddled with the poor portrayal of its people and its potential, riddled with racist attitudes that permeate to information and propaganda about Black men and their "propensity to violence." In addition, Black Americans are continuously deprived of healthy images of Black males. We are constantly fed negative narrative upon negative narrative, and it isn't lost on anyone that this has consequences on our psyche.

It is difficult to navigate all of this without the proper tools, including the one that allows us to practice optimism and to find those silver linings in situations that are less than desirable. This may lead to depression, lack of self-esteem, and lack of will or drive to accomplish anything of value. The best way to counter this is through optimism. "The spirit of optimism that encourages tolerance and growth continues from generation to generation in the Black race. As they become older, they are more likely to transfer such values to their children."[3]

When I think of optimism, the first saying that comes to mind and that I use with my students is, "Thoughts become things." Thus, I encourage them to be the leaders of their thinking vs. letting their circumstances or feelings dictate their thinking because circumstances are temporary and can be changed, and feelings are not always the most reliable.

---

3   https://www.blackphoenixink.org/learned-optimism-in-black-children/

However, I try to have a defined line between "feeling feelings" and redirecting feelings to create/influence positivity and mood. It's important that feelings are not ignored or avoided, and that optimism and silver linings are tapped into once all other feelings have been acknowledged and felt. It's also important to differentiate between healthy optimism and outlook vs. "toxic positivity" and blanketed encouragement because both can be unhelpful.

Making a daily effort to be more optimistic can boost happiness in the long term. We all go through difficult times, but it is important to remain as positive as possible in the face of difficulty. Positive thoughts alone won't change a bad situation, but you can remember that most rough situations pass over time, and what you are experiencing is temporary. Happiness is of our own making, and here are some things we can incorporate into our daily lives to foster more happiness.

1. Focus. It's hard to maintain your focus when it feels like everything is going wrong. Our minds tend to wander away from the present moment and imagine the worst-case scenarios. When you find yourself imagining all the worst outcomes for a situation, bring yourself back to the present. Try to engage your senses in the here and now. What can you feel? What do you hear? Touch something solid to ground yourself in the moment.

    When faced with a difficult situation, ask yourself: "What's next?" Thinking about the next steps you have to take can help clear your mind and help you find your way out of a difficult time. Focus on your goals and future plans. Planning for the future can bring focus to your life. Have positive conversations on goals, ideas, and life. Spend time with people who are excited about life and want to speak about their plans. Being around others who are in a positive mindset helps us to also feel uplifted and motivated to keep going.

2. Practice daily affirmations. Affirmations are positive words of encouragement that boost your feelings of self-worth. It may feel awkward at first to talk to yourself out loud but practicing daily affirmations and saying kind words to yourself can help you change your mental outlook. Try saying, "I am strong" or another positive phrase to yourself in front of the mirror in the morning and remind yourself throughout the day by repeating it.

3. Don't let a roadblock keep you from moving forward. Try to think about how you can make a situation better when you come across a roadblock. What are the possible solutions? What can you do differently next time? Examine and learn from failure. There is no progress without a time to reflect on how to do better. If you fail a test in school, go over the correct answers so you know where you went wrong. Then, you can see how to improve for next time. Life is full of opportunities to learn. Pause and breathe to keep from being overwhelmed. You can always find a silver lining if you are open to seeing it.

4. When someone else is down, say something to bring happiness. Give a compliment or simply ask how they are doing. Create bonds that allow open conversation and create them with people who uplift. These simple acts of kindness help to spread happiness, which extends to you and others.

Forcing yourself to find a silver lining will make you a more compassionate person because it will help you to see things more clearly and objectively. Think of that the next time you find yourself in a rough spot. Try to find joy in the unexpected. Even just making someone smile can bring happiness into your life. The greatest moments in our memories can be spontaneous and unplanned.

Turn negative thoughts around. Whenever you find yourself having negative thoughts, try to find a positive way to change the thought into good energy. Avoid dwelling on the bad. There will always be unhappy moments but what is important is to take what we learn from them to grow. You can always keep moving forward and grow stronger from an unwanted outcome. When things seem to be going poorly, take a step back and view the situation from a different point of view. Look at the situation through some else's eyes for a few minutes. Ask yourself where there is opportunity in the problem. We will be seeing more of this in Weeks 11–12 in discussing how to challenge your negative thoughts.

5. Practice reflecting on your day and thinking about all the good that happened. It can be the smallest event or something exciting. You will end your day on a happy note and with a feeling of gratitude. Remember to be grateful for what you already have. The situation may be terrible, but you have so much going for you already. Remember that. At the end of your day, think back on the good things that have happened, big or small. Ending the day on a positive note can aid with sleep and help you begin the next day with an uplifted mood.

Find balance. Having too much of one thing to eat can make us feel ill, or working more than we relax can be detrimental to our health. It is important to know how to balance everything and align our lives to the happiness we wish to have. Rest. Relax. Take time to do something you enjoy and press the reset button, especially after a stressful day. This will seem familiar as we tackle Weeks 5–6 and learn to create balance.

6. Realize you have the power to change your life. You're not stuck with what you've got going on right now. You can make active choices to improve your situation. Being mindful of your decisions and reactions can make all the difference when cultivating your own joy. No matter how bad the situation seems, remember you have the power to respond to it. Many times, how you react to a problem is key to solving it. Say you have a fight with a friend. Days go by and you haven't made up. You're upset, but you still miss the friendship, so you decide to apologize first. As a result, you and your friend make up. If you had chosen to hang onto your anger, you might not have mended the friendship. This connects to Weeks 51–52: Believe in Your Power to Change Your Life.

Finding the silver lining is all about changing perspectives and being able to actively look for the good in any situation, even if everything seems terrible at the time. Silver linings are not obvious; it takes daily work to reframe the mind to see the goodness within negativity. Once you start finding the good behind any situation, it gets easier to do and creates a positive mindset. We can always choose happiness even in the most difficult moments in our lives. As cliché as this may sound, there is always a light at the end of the tunnel, you just have to open your heart and mind to its existence.

When we practice focusing on the positive and good things in our lives, happiness becomes a natural reaction. We have the power to change our perspective and reframe our minds for a more fulfilling and happy life. It will take daily effort to make lasting change, but you can get there! Start by thinking about your tasks for the day first thing in the morning. How can you make them more enjoyable to get through? Which are the most important to tackle first? What are you going to do to make sure you have some fun in your day?

SPOTLIGHT ON A BLACK ROLE MODEL

Tim Salau, Mr. Future of Work, CEO of Guide, Global Tech Influencer, is a strong believer in overcoming roadblocks and always believing in yourself:

"At the end of the day, you can't let defeat [or] disbelief from the outside kill your own energy. Most of the things that we see around us wouldn't exist if that was the way life goes. The reality is that that's not how life goes. The greatest people, the Kobe Bryants, the Kamala Harrises, the Barack Obamas, they really live another day. They know where they're going. Tell yourself, 'I'm going to keep going there, and I'm going to make sure I get there no matter what.' "

INTROSPECTION:

The 3-to-1 Ratio

Putting more focus on the positive in life, rather than the negative, lends itself to optimism and finding silver linings. A positive outlook allows you to stand tall when things become challenging.

Think of three positives in your day coming up. Write these down. Then, think of one area you'd like to focus your attention on changing. If you do this each day, you'll wind up with three positives and one negative to work on for the day.

WEEKS 11–12: CHALLENGE YOUR NEGATIVE THOUGHTS!

Our thoughts and our beliefs are an integral part of our structure as humans. They define us and our future. Therefore, thoughts have influence over our potential to achieve anything we do. Everything you think, you become. From a very young age, we learn to shape our emotions and feelings, as well as our thinking, and if we don't become conscious of the power of our thoughts, we can affect our entire lifespan indulging in negative thinking, which in turn creates turmoil.

Thoughts can quickly spiral into the negative. According to research,[4] when we're young, we might often find ourselves in repeated patterns of unrealistic negative thinking, called cognitive distortions. "Cognitive distortions are basically thinking mistakes. Learning how to recognize cognitive distortions can make it easier for kids to think more positively and feel better about themselves." You can then grow up with more confidence, and become strong, mentally healthy and equipped young men.

Scientists have also conducted many studies about the power and influence of negative thinking in adults.[5] For many adults, black-and-white thinking—thinking in extremes—is common. Many people wrongly believe that you are either intelligent and successful, or that you are a failure, and many times they absorb this thinking from their environment. Often at a young age, which is why it is crucial to reinforce positive thinking early.

We need to spend more time adjusting our thoughts from negative to positive. And that's easier said than done, but growth mindset, as we previously explained, teaches us that we can improve no matter what our age and circumstance if we can apply the right methods.

---

4 https://childmind.org/article/how-to-change-negative-thinking-patterns/

5 https://www.healthline.com/health/mental-health/black-and-white-thinking#risks

To guide your thinking, you must first be aware of it and aware of what informs it. The inner voice we all develop starts in a variety of places, so I think it's imperative that this section touch on that, so that thinking can be redirected according to that. In the same way youth are encouraged to assess what brings them positive thoughts and feelings, they need to be equipped with tools to assess what brings them the opposite, so they can confront and combat them directly in a way that supports their survival but also allows them to thrive beyond survival.

Negativity is a mental bully we should all stop and confront. Ask yourself if your negative thoughts have any truth to them—and where do these thoughts come from. Why do you think this way about yourself? How do these thoughts affect how you feel about yourself? Examining the root cause and understanding the impact negative thoughts have on you will enable you to confront them and change your way of thinking. As you begin to recognize negative thoughts, you can change them to more positive ones. Start this week.

1. Pay attention to how you feel throughout your day. Does your schoolwork bring you joy? Do the people you surround yourself with uplift your spirit? Focus on what makes you happiest in your day and look forward to those moments. Think about what happiness means to you and bring that into your life. If practicing your free throws on weekends make you happy, do that for yourself. If spending time with your grandparents brings you joy, then enjoy every second of those moments. If happiness comes from your schoolwork, make sure you focus the energy you need into your studies. By focusing your attention on the things that bring you joy, you are more likely to discover new sources of happiness.

2. Change what isn't bringing happiness to your life. Find what can be done to make it more fulfilling. However, know that change is gradual and not instant. Please have patience with yourself through this process. Recognizing that change is not instant will strengthen your resolve and prevent you from falling back into bad habits. Find your peace of mind. Let go of things that do not serve you as you work toward a healthier, happier mindset. Remember you can't control other people, only yourself.

3. Recognize the negative patterns and learn to reframe them. Change the beginning of the thoughts that have a negative connotation. For example, "I'm so stupid," can become, "I'm having a hard time with algebra." Try repeating positive thoughts to yourself when you find yourself engaging in negative thought patterns. "I'm smart enough to get this done"; "I'm strong enough to handle this task." Practice optimism. Instead of telling yourself, "I'll never get over this," try telling yourself, "This may be difficult, but I can get through this." Take the word 'should' out of your thought process. 'Should' inherently makes us feel like it is an obligation and that we need to feel guilty for not doing something. Try changing the 'should' to 'could.' Then decide if it's something you want to do.

4. Stop negative self-talk. Pay attention to the things you tell yourself. Are you saying things like, "I'm never going to get anywhere" or "I have no reason to smile or be happy"? Negativity toward ourselves harms our ability to grow because we lose motivation when we feel unworthy. Try telling yourself, "I got this" or "I can do it" instead. It is important to speak love to ourselves to lift us up, to have faith in our abilities. We often compliment others with

ease, but we do not remember to do the same for ourselves. Focusing on aspects of yourself that you admire will help you feel better about yourself. It helps to remind yourself that you are as important as everyone else in your life. It may feel unnatural at first, but try looking in the mirror and telling yourself things you would like to hear from other people, like, "I am smart. I am strong." This is connected to Weeks 11–12: Challenge your Negative Thoughts.

5. Ask why. Why do you choose to think in the way that you do, and what is a better way to think? What causes your negative thoughts? Are you repeating things in your mind that you hear from the outside world? Who is saying them? Are they valid? Sometimes we repeat things to ourselves without even realizing we're doing it. You will be able to confront negative thoughts once you find what in your environment or experiences caused them to start.

6. Look for solutions as you let go of blame. Practice letting negative thoughts go. When they pop up, just acknowledge them and go about your business with no judgment placed on them. Instead of finding fault, look for solutions. Also, stop worrying. Constant worry can make you spiral into a pattern of negative thoughts. Instead, empower yourself. Recognize where your power lies in the situation. Sometimes it's out of your control, but you always have the choice of how you respond to the situation and that can make a big difference.

7. Stop resisting and start accepting. Resistance can cause more heartache than accepting the events as they unfold. Even though you have the power to change your fate, there are some limitations to what you can do. Sometimes you just have to give up and let go. Knowing when to do this will save you a lot of headaches. Acceptance allows us to stop wallowing in negativity and work toward positive change if we want it.

Andrew Bernard, owner of Make It Dairy-Free, shows how being in sync with your emotions can help you relieve yourself from a bad mood:

"I don't have bad days to be honest with you. Actually, I have bad moments. I'm very much in tune with my feelings. I might look tough, but to be honest with you, I'm very much very in tune with my emotions. I have good emotional intelligence, and I have an awareness about what's going on. So, to be honest, whenever I'm having a moment, I try to think about what I'm feeling first. I let myself stop and think about what the heck is happening to me right now that's making me feel 'off,' per se. And then from that point, I'm very analytical and start breaking it down. If I'm mad, what am I mad about? If I'm mad about [X], what can I do about it? Is there anything I can do about it? How can I fix it? If I'm stressed, what are the things I'm stressed about? [...] I'm very analytical, and I first stop and think about what the problem is, what's going on with me, and where are these feelings resonating from? And once I'm able to home in on where that so-called issue is happening, then I go into Mr. Fix-It mode in a sense, and just try to do whatever I can in order to get back to 'Andrew' again."

INTROSPECTION:

Reframe Critical Self-Talk

It is important for you to have a support system and equally important for you to realize that sometimes you must rely on yourself for validation. You cannot expect your friends to always be there to boost your mood. If you are faced with a situation that is challenging your self-esteem, try the following exercise.

Divide a sheet of paper into four columns. In the first column, write down what the situation is. It might be "I got a D on my physics exam." Then in the second column, write down your initial response. It might be, "Getting a D means I am stupid." In the next column, write down the feelings this statement triggers. You might feel worthless and overwhelmed, for example. In the far-right column, write down the facts about this situation, objectively and with as few emotions as possible. These facts might include, "If I had studied harder for the exam, I probably would have done better" and "I will study harder in the future."

WEEKS 13–14: USE NEGATIVE THOUGHTS TO YOUR ADVANTAGE

Negative thoughts can be repurposed to propel individuals into positive outcomes, especially since the opposite outcome may be detrimental. Teaching this to youth empowers them to take control of their outcomes vs. having them dictated by the helplessness that may lurk in negative thinking patterns. This is crucial, especially when we evolve in a world where we are discouraged to wallow in the negative, but we are not teaching enough this concept: the negative can be useful.

Positive thinking is great, and necessary, but the extreme of positivity also has its perils. We risk the chance of getting badly hurt and scarred with positive thinking because we only expect the best, but we are not prepared for other possible outcomes. Negative thinking to the extreme also leads to a downfall into pessimism and depression, and lack of self-worth. What we are discussing here is how to change the negative into an opportunity for growth. We can learn to acknowledge the negative thoughts, recognize why we are having them, and learn to turn them around. But how do we do that, you ask?

Acknowledging the times where we are unhappy can garner growth. Ignoring unhappiness isn't a solution to dissatisfaction with aspects of your life. It only allows the unhappiness to fester. It's better to acknowledge when something isn't working out for you and to try to make a change. Ask yourself: What are the learning points in this experience?

1. Take the time to examine the unhappy times meaningfully. What can you learn from these unhappy moments? What do these moments reveal that you can work on to change for the better? Is it an internal or external issue? What's happening around you? Do these feelings pop up in one place or setting?

2. Try to find the good in the bad. Seeking the positive that can come out of any situation can improve our mental health. Everything may not always appear as happiness, but we can find and build our own joy through it.

3. Take the day. If you need a day to let negative emotions out, take the day, but move forward tomorrow. We shouldn't stifle our feelings. This can lead to stunted emotional responses and make it harder to connect with those around us. Let the anger or sadness go by writing it down, dancing it out, or through any other form of self-expression that may work for you. Use your creative outlets for release. Paint or draw a picture. Journal about it.

4. Voice it. Speak about the unhappy moments aloud with a close friend or family member, maybe even your pets. There doesn't need to be an in-depth conversation but just the act of speaking it aloud and just having someone listen is validating. Speaking it aloud and releasing it is important to moving on from the experience.

5. Write it! Express your emotions through writing. Try freewriting about them. Take ten minutes and write down what you are feeling and why (if you know why). Don't keep your feelings all bottled up—that will only make them stronger and more pressing.

Roderick Morrow, host of the *The Black Guy Who Tips* podcast, offers how he copes with negative and/or upsetting topics on his show (and in his everyday life):

"Sometimes, the show covers topics that are just rough, whether it's Breonna Taylor or the election of Donald Trump. And so, a big thing that helps is, one, being honest. The second is humor. And I would imagine with a lot of Black people it's like this. We have this undercurrent of gallows humor that is ever present. You could be at a funeral and that one uncle gets up and starts talking and everyone's like, 'Oh, here we go.' So, there's a bit of an undercurrent of humor. And that's how I cope with a lot of stuff—it's the comedy of it. It's like, 'Okay, this is tragic, but this is also ironic or funny in this way.' That's one way I deal with bad days, as far as things go for cheering myself up.

Also, I take breaks. With the show, we work super, super hard. We're very prolific with our output. So, to avoid burnout, it's really important to come up with ideas like, 'Hey, every month let's take a week off.' Or, 'You know what? Let's have an episode where we're just being silly. We're not going to talk about anything too serious.' We have a segment called White People News. It's just about famous celebrities. And, of course, we discuss video games, movies, books, all that kind of entertainment stuff too."

INTROSPECTION:
Challenge Your Inner Critic

Toni Morrison said, "You wanna fly, you got to give up the sh*t that weighs you down."

Talking to yourself in a positive manner when you are feeling down can help lift your mood. Try designing your own self-affirmations by completing the following sentences:

- My friends think I'm fantastic because...
- People tell me I'm great at...
- It makes me feel happy when I...
- I'm proud of...
- It will make my family happy if I...
- I'm the only person I know who...

WEEKS 15–16: SPEND SMARTER

"Money doesn't buy you happiness" is a common saying, but spending your money smartly can increase happiness. In many ways, money is power. The more you have, the more you can do with it. Start this week by saving as much as you can for later when you need it.

Generational wealth building starts with one person breaking the cycle. Also, Black people have a lot of spending/buying power, yet a small slice of the wealth pie, and that has a lot to do with money habits, financial literacy, and generational implications that we have to actively work to shift. How we spend money is important, but how and what we learn about money is truly invaluable.

According to a 2019 report from the Federal Reserve, the typical white family has eight times the wealth of the typical Black family. "The median wealth of white families was $188,200 at the end of 2019, while the median wealth of Black families was $24,100," NBC News wrote.

1. Increase your financial literacy. Find the resources that can help you educate yourself in finances and money so that you don't get caught in the pitfalls of wealth disparity in America. Research[6] shows that "a personal finance education helps students avoid payday loans, have better credit outcomes and reduce private student loan balances and credit card debt, among other things." Many programs exist and are in place now to teach kids and young adults about financial literacy. Banks are now coordinating

6   https://www.americanprogress.org/article/eliminating-black-white-wealth-gap-generational-challenge/
    https://www.cnbc.com/2021/04/06/teaching-financial-literacy-to-kids-can-shrink-the-black-wealth-gap.html
    https://www.binnews.com/content/2020-12-03-this-app-is-helping-black-kids-learn-financial-literacy-save-money/

speaking engagements for bankers to address students on how to save, how to invest, and how to navigate the financial industry on a basic level. There are apps available for download on personal cell phones that are designed to educate users financially, but also help them budget and track their spending as well as their investments. The app Goalsetter for example, designed by African American entrepreneur Tanya Van Court, even offers literacy quizzes and helps young users learn about their spending. We may not be able to undo the wrongs of inequity and the intricate setbacks dealt by years of racial segregation, but we can begin to close the Black and White wealth gap by learning about money and building wealth now through investments.

2. Keep track of your spending. Always be aware of how many purchases you are making in a day, week, or month. Adding up your purchases at the end of the week may surprise you. You'll get a clear look at how much money you really spend, and knowing that can make a big difference when you are considering making purchases in the future.

3. Give yourself a budget. Keeping a budget can help minimize stress because you have a set amount of what you are allowed to spend. Giving yourself a set amount of money for personal spending and bills helps prevent overspending.

4. Break bad spending habits. A bad habit can be impulse-buying or spending money meant for important purchases on miscellaneous items. These can drain your bank account and leave you with less money than you thought you had. If you see something that you want, walk away. If you still want it in a week, you can always go back and buy it. If it's not there, it wasn't meant to be.

5. Always know what you have in your bank account. Checking your bank account daily lets you know what money you have and helps you know when you can spend money as you go about your day.

6. Look for the best deal. Odds are, when you are shopping, you can find a deal or two to keep spending to a minimum. Sometimes you will find a sale if you wait a few days or a week.

7. Start a savings account. For larger purchases you want to make in the future or for college, put a set amount of money into your savings account each week toward those long-term purchase goals.

SPOTLIGHT ON A BLACK ROLE MODEL

Philip Bacon encourages readers to learn how to budget from an early age:

"Young people [often] live for the moment as opposed to thinking about the future and putting away something for the future. I think there's a tension there between what you should do to prepare for your future versus what you want to enjoy right now. I think, number one, people need to get used to budgets. They need to know at all times where their money is going. They need to set some goals for that money."

INTROSPECTION:

Set a Goal

Setting goals is simple if you use the acronym S.M.A.R.T. as a guide. Goals should be Specific, Measurable, Attainable, Relevant, and Time-bound. The best way to start meeting goals is to find small goals you can reach every day. Once you've achieved a set number of these goals, you can set your goals higher, and plan to work harder to achieve them. Start by writing down a list of goals you'd like to achieve tomorrow.

Here's an example of a S.M.A.R.T. goal:

"I will make an extra $15 in allowance by the end of the week, so I can afford to buy a new game. I'll do this by asking for more responsibilities at home, such as watching my little brother and taking out the trash."

S: Specific goal (Raising money for a new game)

M: Measurable ($15)

A: Attainable (A reasonable goal that can indeed be obtained at the end of the week)

R: Relevant (Realistic ways of achieving that goal by babysitting or taking out the trash)

T: Time-bound (Timeline is established, goal to be obtained by end of the week)

Your S.M.A.R.T. goal doesn't have to be money related. There are different kinds of goals that can be set in addition to financial ones. Career, academics, or sports can also be measured. For instance, if your goal is to be a better basketball player, you can set a goal to practice your free throws with a goal of achieving 20 free throws in a row, for 15 minutes a day. It would look like this:

S: Specific goal (Improving at basketball)

M: Measurable (20 free throws in a row)

A: Attainable (15 minutes a day)

R: Relevant (Making the time to practice daily)

T: Time-bound (Aiming to reach that goal by the end of the month)

Another main goal could be to pass an exam. Let's say you are aiming to pass your SAT with high scores—you can set a goal for this as well.

S: Specific goal (Getting a good score on the vocabulary section of the SAT)

M: Measurable (200 words in 2 months)

A: Attainable (Learning 5 words a day for 5 days a week)

R: Relevant (Printing out those words on index cards)

T: Time-bound (2 months)

WEEKS 17–18:
FIND CLARITY
AND PURPOSE

The more research tells us about finding purpose, the more they reassure us that we will live longer, healthier lives when we do, the more we want to seek it out. And yet some of us spend a lifetime trying to determine our life's purpose. Why does it matter? Because purpose is what drives us in the course of our life, what keeps us motivated to achieve goals and feel happy in contributing to something outside of ourselves, even if that purpose involves self-care. What is it that we are we meant to do in life? How can you learn to figure that out, to tap into that which brings you joy and happiness, and use it to make a difference? Finding out your purpose may be tricky, and sometimes it may take long to figure it out, but there are many ways to find the answer early on.

Purpose-driven living drowns out the expectations and "wants" that other people have for you over your life. Dancing to the beat of your own drum first requires that you find your own rhythm.

With all of the messages communicated about Blackness and Black people by non-Black people and outlets, it can be easy to get caught up in "other," "outside," and "external," but clarity and purpose help to keep the focus on self and internal expectations you have of yourself. It drowns out all of the noise. "Because," as entrepreneur Zachary Nunn reminds us, "you owe it to yourself, you should just be yourself. And you should strive to understand and find more of yourself every day, and show up as more of yourself, for yourself, every day. One of the things I hope that my daughter, Emery, learns from me is that authenticity beats out everything else. My hope is that she learns to be an honest and authentic person. You will attract the opportunities, the right relationships, and your body will appreciate you for it, too. And so that's what I really hope."

Finding clarity may ease any anxieties that occur during daily life. It will give direction on how to navigate change and aid in decision-making. Finding clarity can be difficult in a world that's so busy—so, slow down, take deep breaths, and focus from time to time. Being mindful of your surroundings and the reactions of people around you can help you find clarity, too.

Keeping a journal, creating thought lists, and practicing self-reflection can become a kind of daily meditation for stress relief.

1. Ask yourself questions. You can write down answers to your questions to help you find clarity in specific areas of your life. Try this: If you are having trouble deciding on your career or college—or even for simple things such as what to have for dinner—practice asking yourself questions to help you better understand yourself.

2. Journal about your day. This can be the time you relax and reflect on your day. What are the things you enjoy most? Paying attention to how you feel and react to your daily life will help guide you to clarity. What have you accomplished? What have you learned? This will help you realize what you are willing to do and what does not serve your purpose.

3. Create a thought list. This activity can also help you understand yourself better. A thought list is just a list of thoughts you have throughout the day. By creating a thought list, you can create a more intimate relationship with your mind, body, and spirit, which will help you to be better aligned to your wants, desires, or goals. Declutter your mind: Do a mind dump on paper to get all your thoughts out. You can go back and find patterns, whether good or bad, and decide how you can change things for

the better. This can help you find focus. What do you have that no longer brings you joy or serves you? Look at your daily life and remove anything that is not adding value to it. For instance, minimize the commitments you agree to in a day. Another way to declutter your life is not to take on too many commitments. Taking on more than you may have time for can cause added stress and take time away from your priorities.

4. Declutter your space. Sometimes a messy space is reflective of a messy mind. Cleaning your room will help to refresh and refocus your life. Start with the area right around you and move through your living spaces, separating things into piles of what you want to keep and what you need to get rid of. Then, put things away. Do a little of this every day to keep your room neat and tidy. Declutter your closet or anything that needs to be refreshed and renewed. Rid your room and living spaces of anything that doesn't see any use.

5. Add activities and hobbies into your schedule. Find things to do that stretch your skillset and practice them. Make time in your day for some fun. It's important to ask yourself what holds value in your life and what brings progressive happiness. You can try giving up some of the things that don't bring happiness, too. However, it's important to realize that there are certain tasks we must all do, no matter how much we dislike them.

Sometimes it takes several tries to find out what you want in life, whether it's in your career or personal life. It's okay not to know right away, but try anyway. Keep trying until you get it right, and experiment! If you are unsure of what you want to do, try different things until you find what you enjoy.

SPOTLIGHT ON A BLACK ROLE MODEL

Marlon Peterson, author of *Bird Uncaged: An Abolitionist's Freedom Song*, demonstrates how finding meaningful activities and hobbies can help you through rough patches in your life:

"I think that as writers, as artists, as poets, [creativity] is one of the things that we can lift up more within our young folks, within our community, for people to be able to express themselves. Because there's a lot of pent-up agony in a lot of our folks. And it comes out in very counterproductive ways. We see it on the news. We got to create the spaces for our folks to be able to release those untold stories, those pains."

INTROSPECTION:

Create a Life Vision

Barack Obama said, "Change will not come if we wait for some other person or some other time. We are the ones we've been waiting for. We are the change that we seek." Imagine the life you'd like to be living in twenty-five years. Ask yourself: What will I be doing? Where will I live? How will I spend my time? Who do I want to spend time with? Freewrite for a couple of minutes to see what vision of your future you can create. Remember to focus on big goals in this exercise.

Alternatively, you can create a vision board here as well. Writing things down is a good start, but the images and collaging really allow for the vision to be visualized. Here are the steps for a vision board:

1. Imagine a clear goal. Get clear about what you want before you start cutting out pictures. What matters most to you? Is it money? Is it helping your community? Do you want to start a project that would help other people? Maybe it's being a motivational speaker? It helps to write down the goals or determine, as you start looking through the pictures, what speaks more to you before you even grab your scissors.

2. Use 80 percent pictures, 20 percent words. After all, "a picture is worth a thousand words." Time to get out your magazines or use an online program, like Pinterest or Canva. There is a free version of Canva, as well as a paid version, Canva Pro. I encourage you to create and use your digital vision board as the wallpaper for your

phone, tablet, or computer if you have one. That way, it's visible often and serves as constant encouragement.

3. Organize your goal by quarter. Divide your vision board into four quadrants, so you can chunk it into smaller goals. Maybe the first section is for the big picture goal, with the large house and the two cars and a swimming pool. The second could be a step below that, a posh apartment or penthouse in the city. Maybe the third quadrant is where you mostly see yourself succeeding in your career, and the fourth is the very next promotion you see yourself getting at work toward that final goal. These quadrants can be different desires and wants you have for different aspects of your life: work, family, leisure, and the future. It's up to you.

4. Put your vision board on display. If you can't see it, you can't imagine it, and you can't make it happen. Collect magazines, pictures you find even in junk mail, and if you don't have any you can always get scraps from thrift stores or ask your family for extra magazines they're no longer reading. But you may also choose to build your board online, using Pinterest or other apps that allow you to post photos. The idea is for you to gather images of experiences you want to achieve in your life and use those. If your passion is soccer, or basketball, then photos of those experiences may be perfect. Photos of an athlete crossing the finish line, or a chef living their dream of building chocolate sculptures, or someone sailing or surfing. Even if it's a picture of a person relaxing in a bathtub, overlooking the mountains. Whatever your heart desires goes on the board. See yourself there enough that it becomes almost a reality to you.

5. Create an action plan. This could take any shape or form, but you may consider writing down your plan into a journal entry, or just simple bullet points. What is it you love to do? Where are you at your happiest? What are you passionate about? You can freewrite about how you visualize yourself: what does that look like ideally? If money were no object, where would you be right now? What first step can you take toward that goal? This action plan can also be unwritten if you can prepare yourself for the right relationships, being in the right place at the right time, and talking to other people who seem to have found their purpose: What are they doing? Why do they like it? How does that relate to your experience? Ask for advice or meet those people for lunch every now and then in a sort of mentor-mentee relationship. Offer to help or volunteer if you can with their organization or be bolder with the organizations you love. What do those look like and how might you fit in them? This can help you learn more about yourself, about the subjects you love, and you may find your purpose through that experience.

WEEKS 19–20: IMAGINE HAPPINESS

Too often, negative aspects of Blackness are broadcast in the mainstream and Black joy is not. Images of Black male youth especially have rarely, up till this day, captured true happiness. Dr. Huey P. Newton said in his past as an activist, that he did "not expect the media to create positive Black male images." In mediums around the country, and around the world, we have seen Black people portrayed in negative light, perpetuating subtle ideas of violence and tragedy, poverty, and suffering as part of our genetic makeup. Many have bought into this idea, and worse. How we can combat this is through our own re-enaction and imagination of happiness.

If Black male youth can imagine happiness, then they can experience and create it, which is vital and adds dimension, depth, and balance to the Black experience. If you can take pride in who you are, in yourself and in your values, your happiness can start there. A study led by psychology researchers at Michigan State University and published online in a 2011 issue of *Cultural Identity and Ethnic Minority Psychology* found that "African American people who identify more strongly with their racial identity are generally happier." There is a lot to be said for feeling love and joy among your kin, especially in a world that barrages you with negativity. It feels safe, and it feels good to share new experiences with your family, to get love and praise from your grandparents and cousins who show up for you at your weekend games, to sleep under the stars together with your friends and learn about constellations. When was the last time you got a good belly laugh from a joke your uncle said at the dinner table?

There is more than one way to be happy in life. Happiness can have many different meanings for every individual. This week, the focus will be to explore what happiness means to you. How does it manifest itself in your life?

Use your imagination to create the life you seek. Creating the life we want in our minds can help us have focus to form a plan toward that vision. Our lives may not unfold the way we plan, and opportunities may arise that change its course, but the important part is having the courage to go after your dreams. This week, you'll imagine the future of your dreams and start making it a reality.

1.   Imagine the future you want. It is the first step to making it a reality. Your future is as big as your imagination, but you can start small. Break down your future into five-year blocks and imagine where you'll be in 5, 10, 15, or 20 years. What does your future look like to you? Take a few minutes to imagine the future of your dreams. You may even want to write it down to remind yourself when you lose sight of your goals. The present unfolds to the future slowly, and looking back, you can see your goals coming together. This could be something you also choose to do as a vision board, to help you see a clear image of what that future looks like and all the things you want in it.

2.   Imagine the steps for your goals. Write out a plan or list of goals to achieve. Taking bigger goals and breaking them down into daily, weekly, monthly, or yearly objectives is important. What steps do you need to take to achieve your goals? We can easily become overwhelmed sometimes by how big we think our dreams are. Breaking them down into manageable tasks makes them more achievable. You may even consider writing this as a S.M.A.R.T. goal, breaking it down how we did it earlier.

3. Put into the world what you want to receive back. If you give off positive energy through any situation, the universe will respond in kind. The world might feel like it is crumbling around you, but there is something positive to be found through it. Hold onto that and keep moving forward. When you find yourself acting or talking out of negativity, stop yourself and ask how you can change. How can you be more positive? Try not to let fear keep you from going after everything you want out of life or from following your heart. Negative emotions get in the way of pursuing your goals and are one of the reasons we may choose not to do something that could be fulfilling.

4. Imagine the finish line. How will it feel when you reach your goals? Take a few minutes to imagine that feeling in your body. Tell yourself you will get to your goals, and it will give you the courage to start. We need to feel confident in ourselves to start taking the steps we need to take to achieve our wildest dreams.

5. When an opportunity arises, take it. Life gives you opportunities that may lead you away from your initial goals. It's up to you to recognize when an opportunity is worth the risk involved in giving up your main goal. You'll need to learn to be flexible and follow new chances for success in different places than you thought you'd find them.

6. Don't overthink. Overthinking can be the one thing to keep you from feeling happiness in your accomplishments. When you get that A- in Spanish, just celebrate that you brought the grade up; don't worry so much that it wasn't perfect. Apply what you have learned when you think you could have done better, instead of telling yourself you did terribly. You accomplished the goal, celebrate you. Tell yourself you did it and be happy with the progress you've made.

7. Constantly allow yourself to learn and grow. When life presents you with something that looks like failure, take it as an opportunity to improve. Fail forward, like the F.A.I.L. acronym suggests: First Attempt In Learning. Acknowledge what you can do better and apply what you learn to the next experience. Constantly allowing ourselves to learn is the catalyst of growth. Grow wiser and more confident.

One of the best ways to seek and find happiness within your life is to stop trying to be someone you're not or living for the benefit of others. **Zachary Nunn**, founder of Living Corporate, gives some advice of his own on living your truth:

"Live as authentically as you can every day. I think it's really easy to get in situations, especially in the corporate space, where Black and brown people are often encouraged to play these games where we code switch or hide parts of who we are, to be better accepted. But the reality is that white people, and those just in the power majority, they see you, speaking either in the Queen's English or in your localized dialect [...] They're going to treat you a certain way, irrespective of how much you try to assimilate."

INTROSPECTION:

One Thing a Day

To increase your courage and willingness to try new things, try stepping out of your comfort zone. Happiness is outside your comfort zone! Only when you leave your bubble can you measure your degree of happiness.

Talk to people you wouldn't talk to normally. Practice being in uncomfortable situations. For example, if you are shy, try putting yourself out there more. Talk to the waitress at your next meal out. Find low-risk situations you can practice at before big events. This can also connect to Weeks 31–32: Get Out of Your Comfort Zone.

WEEKS 21–22:
GO AFTER LIFE!

You only get one life to live, so it's your responsibility to make the best of it. Not for your family, your teachers, your peers, or society—but for you. Everyone was created with a gift for the world, and the only way to uncover it is to explore yourself and figure out what you're good at, what you enjoy, and what makes you feel fulfilled and purpose-driven. Going after life contributes to that self-exploration, so it's essential for Black male youth to have the freedom to do so, if they are truly going to mature and grow into the adults they are meant to be and share their individual gifts with the world. Otherwise, going after the life others predetermined you are supposed to have or are capable of having may likely leave you unfulfilled and will leave the world lacking. Black male youth deserve to lead lives of the former, not the latter.

Life is for the living, so get out there and do what you want to do. Live fully and with joy. Share that joy with loved ones. Fill your life with fond memories and fulfilling goals. What do you want to accomplish for yourself? What have you realized about the life you are living? Hopefully, you are living it fully and lovingly.

Knowing what your goals are and finding your purpose in life can be intimidating, especially in a society that promotes certain expectations. The expectations for young Black men are typically low. You're likely not to get pushed very hard to make something better of yourself, so you'll need to rely on yourself to want more out of life than what is expected for you. You can do anything you set your mind to. Remember that you are on your own journey, and no one else can dictate your life but you.

1.   Think about your passions in life. Write them down. What brings you joy? What are you good at? How can you build a life centered around these passions? When exploring your passions, ask yourself: Who? What? When? Where?

Why? Knowing these details can help you calibrate your life so that you treat it as an adventure. Does music bring you joy? DO you find yourself most alive when teaching younger kids how to play and understand video games? Are you told that you are very good at organizing events for your community? Listen to what your peers, your elders, and people in your environment in general are telling you about yourself. Often, we find our passion through others' feedback. Maybe there is a career for you in local politics or development with an organization through that passion you didn't realize you had.

2. Explore different avenues to find what is right for you. You may not find it immediately, but it's important not to give up when an idea falls through. Right now, you should be exploring different interests and seeing what makes sense for you to do in the future. Are you good at math? Does biology interest you? Find what you can be passionate about and pursue what's fun and interesting to you. Don't be afraid to switch paths if the one you're on is not something you love completely.

3. Pay attention to what you are good at doing. Your talents may lead you down a different path than you envisioned, so it's important to pay attention to what feels right. You'll know you're on the right track when you find something to do that comes easy to you and you enjoy doing it. This connects to listening to feedback around you. Sometimes we excel at a task that others can't do or are unable to do, and this is where your purpose might lie.

4. Pay attention to what brings you happiness when you're doing it. You may be working toward a goal that brings more stress than happiness, so look for times when you enjoy work. When you do what you love, time passes quickly, and you lose yourself in the process of what you are doing because you feel right doing it. There may be parts of work that we don't particularly enjoy because they cause us stress and anxiety, and we might be tempted to quickly abandon the task. It's important to note that even though those moments may not feel joy-filled, they challenge us, teach us important skills, and help us grow. Young entrepreneurs, for example, may find their work enjoyable but many may not care for customer-facing opportunities, or may not favor the retail side of their job. And yet they cannot just throw in the towel and give up because those moments cause discomfort. Instead, they charge ahead because they know this is an opportunity for growth. Those moments are often smaller pieces of a larger pie, and the larger pie is what brings happiness. As Frederick Douglass said, "If there is no struggle, there is no progress."

5. Remember that good things take time and don't happen overnight. Every process can be broken down into steps, so look to take small steps at first. Before you know it, you'll be running along quickly. Most things in life are a work in progress, and it's important not to let the first obstacle prevent you from making your dream a reality.

Finding your passion(s) in life is not necessarily a linear path.

"I'm from Cleveland, Ohio. I started my career in finance, but I was always interested in doing work that was more meaningful, maybe more purpose-driven. I used my background in finance as kind of a leverage point to do work that was more interesting. And so, that led me to microfinance, which is an industry kind of designed around banking for low-income populations. And that's where I started working outside the US, not just in Africa, but Asia, and the Middle East.

"And that's where I got exposed to agriculture. In continents like Africa, 70 percent of the workforce is devoted to agriculture, but they're not very well-supported [and] don't have access to the tools and the resources that farmers in, let's say, North America have access to. And so, I thought that would be a good place to focus, which ultimately led to Hello Tractor, which led to me moving to Nigeria. And now six years later, I'm here in Kenya doing that work in our second office here in Nairobi."

—**Jehiel Oliver**, founder of Hello Tractor

INTROSPECTION:

Before You Die

Make a list of goals you'd like to accomplish before you die. Another way to do this exercise is to ask yourself: What would you do if you only had a year to live? Be specific, but don't rule out goals because you think they may be impractical. In the next column, answer the question: How might achieving this goal change my life for the better? In a third column, rate each goal on its meaning to you, where 10 is very meaningful and 0 is not meaningful at all. Remember these words by Muhammad Ali: "If they can make penicillin out of moldy bread, they can sure make something out of you."

Think about the male role models in your life and ask yourself who they are and how they started out.

WEEKS 23–24: LIVE YOUR VALUES

Values guide a person's life and serve as a moral compass. Without them, discerning right from wrong and making effective decisions may be difficult. Values precede what you will stand for to ensure you don't simply fall for nothing. Values influence our thoughts and our actions and say what we are on the surface to people who are curious about us.

Values can be broken down into categories: individual values or how you show up in your everyday life, relationship values pertaining to how you relate to others, organizational values or what your organization stands for out in the world, and societal values or how your organization relates to society. In short, values are principles that help you navigate life on a daily basis.

Determining your core values and living them is important. Living your values is important because it makes you a more genuine person and helps you build a life you feel comfortable in. It can be hard to determine your core values, but you can start by creating a list of them that you hang somewhere you can see it regularly.

To determine your core values, you should start with a list of existing values and figure out which ones you find yourself most drawn to. *Psychology Today*[7] also recommends talking to other people, preferably older people in your life who can offer insight and advice.

Question yourself constantly about whether you are acting in line with what matters most to you in life. Are you being kind? Honest? Whatever reflects your core values is how you should act.

---

7   https://www.psychologytoday.com/us/blog/changepower/201811/6-ways-discover-and-choose-your-core-values

1. What are your values? This can be a hard question to answer, so take the time this week to examine what is important to you. What brings purpose to your life? What do you feel is wrong? Know when/what things don't align with your values. There is power in saying no, and when something does not align with you, don't let it dictate your decisions.

2. When making an important decision, review your values. Our values can be the basis of our character. When important moments arrive, our values can lead us to the answer that will reflect positively. It will bring joy and fulfillment, not confusion and uncertainty.

3. Align your daily routine to your values. If you value good health, make time to exercise. If you value your friendships, make time to nurture them. Do what feels right to you. When you wake up in the morning, take a few minutes to reflect on your values and how you can live them that day. Then, in the evening, check back in with yourself to see if you were successful. If you value financial freedom, did you spend the day working toward that goal or reviewing your plan? Did you remind yourself to follow the steps you'd established for yourself? If you value time with family, then did you show up for your grandparents and relatives who needed you that day?

4. Renegotiate relationships. Make a list of people in your life who lead you astray from your core values, and ask yourself: "How can I renegotiate these relationships?" This can be tough to do, because in some cases, renegotiating may mean to sever ties. Not everyone will share your values, and if they don't, they won't always understand your drive. If

you value financial security, for example, you may find that some relationships work against that value. A relationship that demands you constantly give your time and energy and money, friends that insist you spend freely when going out and hanging out even when they know your values, will need to be rethought. It's difficult, but this may call for an honest conversation that may end up in the backburner. You will have to reprioritize and put that value first.

SPOTLIGHT ON A BLACK ROLE MODEL

Writer **Geoffrey Philp** regularly reminds himself of his core values:

"Everything starts with a purpose. Once you realize your purpose, then everything else falls into place. It's about finding that purpose within you. Then all other things will follow. As a writer, I ponder, 'How can my stories and poems impact my readers the way Bob Marley's songs did? What is my purpose within my ancestral, national, and family tradition/lineage? How can I be self-reliant in all of that? How will I eat? How will my children eat? How will I make sure that while I'm writing that I'm keeping a roof over my head?' "

This can also be connected to Weeks 17–18: Finding Clarity and Purpose. Throughout this book, you will also learn about values, which is relevant for readers like you as you step out boldly.

INTROSPECTION:
Be True to Yourself

Being true to yourself allows you to speak up and stand up for what you believe in. It doesn't mean you ignore the advice of others; you should still hear them out but do so knowing you can take a stand for what you believe is right no matter what anyone else is doing. When you start being true to yourself, you'll get a gut instinct that will tell you that you are acting in line with your values.

"I prefer to be true to myself, even at the hazard of incurring the ridicule of others, rather than to be false and to incur my own abhorrence."

—Frederick Douglass

Start each day with the affirmation, "I believe in myself." After you've done this for a while, you'll start to convince yourself that you really do have faith in yourself, and your actions will follow. In your journal, reflect: What are some questions you can ask yourself to recall and reinforce your core values?

WEEKS 25–26: DEVELOP AN ATTITUDE OF GRATITUDE

Gratitude can show us what we already have and keep us living in the present. Being thankful for what we already have in life keeps us from becoming cynical and feeling cheated out of life. It increases our levels of happiness and makes us see the world differently. Research has even proven the effect of gratitude on our health. People who express gratitude regularly experience less depression, sleep better, and have less anxiety. Doctors have even correlated gratitude with lower levels of inflammation and better heart health in patients who live a life of gratitude.

In your goal to walk boldly into the world, you will want to develop an attitude of gratitude not just for your health, but also to increase the flow of positive energy between you and others. When you are grateful and you show it, you make others feel better about themselves and you make them feel valued. This can only create better conditions for everyone, and soon they will be modeling their gratitude from your experiences. Try it!

1. Practice gratitude. Gratitude can improve our self-worth. When we are thankful for the gifts in our lives, we tend to be happier. Finding things to be thankful for isn't so hard to do. They can be simple things, like having a hot breakfast before going to school and understanding that many kids in the world don't have those simple things to be thankful for. Make gratitude a part of your day. Every day, think of four things you are grateful for. You can even write them down in a gratitude journal to remind yourself that there are things in life to be thankful for. Start your mornings speaking gratitude. Tell yourself what you are thankful for. Make a list of things. Speaking aloud positivity can help anchor your day in motivation. End your day with gratitude. Reflect on your day and think about moments you appreciate.

2. Be mindful of what you pay attention to throughout your day. What do you notice when you are just walking down the street or driving? Are you being positive or negative? Are you listening and paying attention? Having gratitude as our attitude forces us to be more present. Really listen to your friend in need and give strong advice. Pay attention to how people treat you and vice versa.

3. Be on the lookout for happy moments in your day. Acknowledge them when they occur. When you have a happy moment, memorize the feeling in your body. Really focus on how it feels. Keep that feeling in mind for when you're feeling down.

4. Tell people "Thank you" when they do or say something kind. Something as simple as acknowledging a kindness can help shift your perspective and change the way you feel.

5. Smile. It sends a message to your body that you're happy and lets others around you feel your joy, too. Start greeting people. This action will not only uplift your mood, but it can positively impact another person as well.

6. Give compliments. Giving compliments can lift your mood, increase self-worth, and create the basis for positive relationships. It lets the other person know they are valued and appreciated and spreads joy. It feels good to give a compliment. Try it this week.

   - Make the compliments specific to the person. If you see your friend this week, give them a compliment that highlights something specific about them. For example, you can say, "I like what you said in history class. It made me think more about the topic we were discussing."

- Share the reason why you gave the compliment. Try not to give a generic compliment like, "You look beautiful today" or "You're very smart." Give a more specific reason why you are giving them a compliment.

- Don't be shy! Compliments are never a bad idea. If you have something positive to share with someone, tell them. It can make a difference in their day and their thinking. You can even extend compliments to strangers if you see something you like about them. You never know, you might make a new friend.

- Don't make the compliment a double-edged sword. Say a compliment without the 'but' attached. For example, if you expected your coworker to help you with a task and they did do it, but the work is not to the level of perfection that you expected (maybe they made mistakes or maybe it's not as neat as you hoped for), consider just saying thank you. Be grateful for the help and let them know you truly are.

7. Don't forget to extend kindness to yourself. Give yourself compliments on your accomplishments, your style, or your strength. There are so many ways you are deserving of recognition and are worthy. Stop the negative thoughts in their tracks. We should all pay attention to the way we speak to ourselves. It is so easy to be courteous with others, but oftentimes we are not kind to ourselves. We might make a mistake or find something we do not like, so we tell ourselves

we are not worthy in some way. This is a concept we visit in Weeks 49–50 when learning how to treat yourself as a friend.

8. Give back! Volunteer your time to help someone. Giving some of your time to help another can make a bigger difference in their lives than you think. Find an organization to donate your time or money. Research a cause you would like to support and be a part of the events. Find out what you can do within your own community. Giving back to your own community is a great way to help make change, even if it is on a one-to-one level. Share resources and knowledge through social media. We are all learning together. Anything you may learn can be helpful in someone else's learning.

9. Embrace kindness and empathy. Kindness and empathy bring happiness and gratitude to your life. They open you up to a more positive outlook. Practice empathy while at work or school. It is easy to just focus on our perspective instead of trying to understand why someone may feel or think the way they do. These days, kindness and empathy are in short supply. When you find yourself in conversation with a friend who, for example, tells you they're struggling with time management because of something deeply personal going on in their lives, it is okay to stop and listen to them. It's okay to give them space, and encourage them with friendship, and offer help. Society tells us that people must learn to check their personal issues and leave them at home, but that trains us to neglect self-care and empathy. Reach out to your peers, and show them the power of empathy and kindness, and they will learn to pass it on.

Whenever stand-up comedian **Hennessy Williams III** feels sad, he turns to practicing gratitude.

"It took me years [...] to just understand that I should probably practice the art of gratefulness. What do I have that other people don't that I honestly didn't earn? To me, those are the things you should be 100 percent grateful for, the things that kind of fell into your lap. If you go out and you get a paycheck from your job, you earn your paycheck. You're not really grateful for the paycheck. You're grateful for the job because they didn't have to give you the job. To me, it always has been like, 'Okay. What is out of my power, but has been a blessing anyway?' Family. Who I have is my family. I'm also grateful for being good at stand-up comedy [...] The ability to connect with people from a humorous standpoint and kind of meld minds for a moment because that's what joke-telling is. Being able to connect with somebody in their mind for just a split moment to just know what another person feels for a second."

Practice Self-Care and Gratitude

Find a self-care routine that works for you, whether it is getting nine hours of sleep each night or making sure you look good when you go out. Self-care can be a lot of easy little things that don't take up much time, like watching your favorite animal videos, or taking ten minutes to read a book that gives you pleasure or that teaches you new things. Make a list of things you are grateful for and keep it in a place where you can easily retrieve it when you need it. Another facet of this is practicing gratitude daily, like starting each day with two to three things you're thankful/grateful for and recalling those things when times get tough throughout the day.

WEEKS 27–28:
STAY MINDFUL

Being mindful in our daily lives allows us to grow and learn. Mindfulness has increasingly become an integral part of our daily lives, with schools around the country spending a few minutes in the morning to help students focus their minds and achieve their goals. There are schools that have even begun to replace detention with mindfulness sessions, meditation and yoga, and noticed an improvement in behavior as a result. We are becoming more and more aware of what meditation can do for the mind, how it can influence our behavior and our response to stressful situations, and we are now sharing different techniques, teachings, and practices with each other. Black young men are often so driven, however, by their quest for success, that they forget themselves in the process. Meditation can help ground you, give you clarity, and help sharpen your focus. You're clearing your mind, and wiping your hard drive clean so that you can move forward.

We can find patterns and new ideas by being present in every situation. If you find yourself daydreaming a lot, this week will challenge you to pay attention to what's happening all around you. By focusing on the present, you'll become more aware of the opportunities that are opening to you right now and what changes you want to make for your future.

1. Pay attention to what you choose to focus on in your life. We can put our energy to good use or be wasteful by paying attention to a negative experience. This can be connected to our previous discussion about positive thinking, and our conversation about values. If what you want is a better quality of life, a better outlook, then surrounding yourself with the wrong kind of people is certainly not the right decision. The more time you spend putting your energy toward those things that serve you and your interests, the more you increase your chances at reaching your goals. If,

instead, you are caught up in the negative experiences, you run the risk of derailing your own future.

2. Be mindful of your daily routines. Sometimes having a daily routine can be grounding, or it can be something you change up every so often to get yourself out of a rut. For example, if you always eat breakfast as soon as you get up, try taking a walk or a jog before you eat to get a chance to see what's going on in the world outside your home first thing in the morning. If you are feeling as though you do not have any motivation, try changing your routine. It's a small action, but you may be surprised by what can inspire you. Make positive changes for yourself. Maybe start the day with music that lifts your mood. Do more of what makes you happy, and don't tell yourself you can't because of outside opinions.

3. Pay attention to any bad habits. When we are mindful of our daily routines, we can see habits that do not serve us. Habits may be hard to break, but the first step is to realize it to change it. When you find yourself about to engage in a bad habit, stop yourself and ask what else you could do instead of the action you're considering.

4. Spend time with loved ones. Be mindful of how much time you spend with your family and friends. Sometimes you must be away from them, but they are important to your sense of self. Find a balance that makes you joyful and cultivate those relationships. Spending less time on social media and more time with loved ones will improve your mood. Come back down to the real world; social media can help create a fabricated world full of vanity and material fixations, a world in which your favorite athletes, artists,

or influencers in general are living largely. This can often lead to depression or inflict a sense of low achievement. But when you break away from it, you can appreciate your life more. Consider contacting your family and friends outside of social media. Say you get a notification that it's someone's birthday, pick up the phone and give them a call instead of liking their picture, commenting, or posting on their wall.

5. Put in effort to be present. Time can easily get away from us, and in the age of technology, it is not easy to remain present with our friends and family. If you find yourself daydreaming, focus instead on the here and now. Allow yourself to really be present at any given moment, especially if you are with others. Pay attention to your surroundings and the people talking to you. Make a greater effort to engage with others so they feel valued.

Being mindful might require you to take breaks from social media and ditch your phone. Social media can be both amazing and detrimental. You can have friends from all around the world. Connecting with others has never been easier, but spending too much time on your phone can affect your mental health. Spending too much time on your smartphone separates you from the world around you and distracts you from what's going on. This week, try a social media detox and see what happens. Weeks 39–40: Develop Healthy Habits will also connect to this passage.

1. Give yourself more time for sleep. Being on your phone before bed keeps your brain awake and active, which makes it harder to fall asleep. Getting enough sleep is important because it helps you recharge. Instead of spending extra time at night on your phone, spend the time unwinding by reading a book, meditating, or just resting in gratitude with

your eyes closed. You'll find you get better sleep and are more rested in the morning.

2. Get your body moving. Many people spend more time in front of the screen for work, school, or even at home. It's important to minimize this and get your body doing more than just sitting. Exercise will help you feel stronger and more focused, and it's good for your body to move.

3. Uplift your mood. Taking breaks from social media can be one of the best habits for your mental health. A lot of what is posted on social media platforms is the best parts of life. It is basically a highlight reel that can make us feel like our life isn't great in comparison. Taking a social media break will allow you time to do things you might not have tried if you were looking at the phone. You will have more time on your plate to focus on other things, like taking that class you always wanted, or spending a half hour outside in nature, taking in those scenes you don't normally take in when staring at your phone. It allows you to experience life more.

4. Bring the focus back to you. Social media has everyone looking outside of themselves, and we should all remember to bring the focus back to our lives to be present. Keep track of how much time you spend on social media and place a limit on yourself. If you find you're having a hard time following those limits, you can download an app that will limit your time for you.

5. Set up social media-free days. On these days, don't check your pages at all. Maybe it's Sunday. Maybe it's the whole weekend. Have social media-free zones in your home—at the dinner table, for example. Consider using an app that helps you set your social media time, so that it automatically blocks you from having access to social media. You can also put someone else in charge to monitor your usage and offer to do the same for them. Severing ties with social media is you reclaiming your time and choosing to prioritize what you feel is most important. Hopefully, that's you!

SPOTLIGHT ON A BLACK ROLE MODEL

If you lead a spiritual life, you have a community and a model for how to commune with yourself and your higher spirit through prayer. Mindfulness is more of a meditation practice, a constant reminder to remain grounded, developing the right mindset for opportunities.

"I didn't have role models until I got to prison and found God. Before I learned how to pray, my role models were drug dealers, people that drove a Cadillac or a Mercedes and wore big chains. Then I found God and started praying and meditating. I learned in prison how to treat a woman. I learned in prison how you're supposed to treat your family. I learned in prison how you're supposed to be respectful. I learned in prison how you're supposed to be right. I saw in prison men who changed their lives through prayer."

—**Albert Campbell**, executive member of The Circle of Brotherhood

INTROSPECTION:

My Wins

You can help boost your self-confidence by recalling past events where you felt self-assured and strong and by relying on the feelings that arise in you. To practice, recall a time when you felt especially self-confident, and then recall how the moment felt in your body. Then, project that self-confident feeling outward. This is exactly what we discussed on Weeks 1–2 when touching on the Shot of Confidence.

"Success is to be measured not so much by the position that one has reached in life as by the obstacles which he has overcome while trying to succeed."

—Booker T. Washington

WEEKS 29–30:
FACE STRESS HEAD ON

Stress is connected to health and quality of life, so it is important for the average person to know how to manage and handle it well. Unfortunately, with microaggressions, racism, oppression, and other negative factors associated with being a person of color, we often experience a greater deal of stress simply due to the hue of our skin. In fact, stress has been shown in research to be a great factor in the detriment of Black people. Stress forces the release of a hormone in our bodies called cortisol. According to research, "cortisol temporarily increases energy production required for immediate survival—like running from a bear or escaping a house fire. For the average person, cortisol levels begin high in the morning and taper off as the day progresses, fluctuating appropriately. In African American men living in socioeconomically depressed communities, cortisol levels start and remain high—the bear is always chasing; the smoke alarm's always screeching."[8]

Cortisol is also related to early-onset diabetes, which constantly threatens African Americans. "About 13 percent of African Americans age 20 and older have been diagnosed with diabetes, according to the American Diabetes Association. About 9 percent of all Americans are diabetic, according to the Centers for Disease Control and Prevention."

"There are two kinds of worries—those you can do something about and those you can't. Don't spend any time on the latter."

—Duke Ellington

---

8   https://www.huffpost.com/entry/is-stress-killing-black-men_b_58c2b6f8e4b0c3276fb783c8

Worry can lead to debilitating anxiety if we let it take over our minds. The mind is a powerful part of being human, and it controls how we perceive the world around us. We choose to see the possibilities in either a positive or negative light. The stress we are facing every day easily takes a toll. As we just talked about mindfulness, this is a perfect opportunity to put this concept into practice. We can learn to control our level of stress and manage it in order to take care of ourselves, physically and mentally. This week, let's work on moving away from worry's negativity and toward a more brilliant world.

1. Think of solutions instead of negativity. We can be consumed in the moment by fear, anger, or other emotions, but take a moment to collect yourself. Breathe, go outside, remove yourself from the situation and try to think about how to fix or change it.

2. Do what helps you to de-stress. Whether it's taking a few minutes to unwind with a fidget spinner, Wacky Track, stress putty, Pop It fidgets, or taking a run to jog off some extra energy, find the thing you can do that will help you untangle the tension in your body. Take the time to fit manageable methods of calming into your routine when you are stressed. Have you found ways to de-stress this week? What have you noticed about your daily routine that may be causing stress?

3. Talk about your worries with someone you trust. Sometimes just speaking your worries can allow you to see solutions and feel supported. Young Black men, in particular, are vulnerable and less likely to reach out when they are in crisis. It's important that you find supportive people you can lean on when overwhelming situations arise and everything feels hopeless.

4. Recognize patterns and how to address them. Once you find patterns in your life that cause you more stress, you can work on solutions for them. If you notice an increase in your level of stress after your morning commute, consider ways in which you can make the journey more digestible. Relaxing music, or maybe a podcast or program that keeps you focused so that you engage less with the stress. If the daily news you consume is agitating you, it's okay to reduce the flooding of information simply by muting notifications on your phone, for example. You can then make changes and form better habits to make your life as stress-free as possible.

5. Realize it is okay to feel what you feel and work through it. We should validate our own feelings and not let outside forces influence the way we react to something. There are unhealthy reactions we can always work on to be better, but our initial feelings are valid. You should take the time to examine the reason behind the emotion.

6. Take a deep breath. Take moments to calm yourself before you decide to express how you feel to someone else. Sometimes when you become so overwhelmed by emotion in the moment, you may not know what the core issue is and why. Give yourself some time to process the situation and how you feel so the conversation will be beneficial for both parties.

7. Be kind to yourself. Acknowledge what is causing the frustration and stress in your life to understand why. We can be our greatest critic, and this can cause added stress. Previously, we've discussed the importance of showing kindness and compassion, and it's easier to do with others than it is with ourselves. Remember to treat yourself with respect. It is okay to rest, it is okay to relax and decompress and to have fun. It is okay to laugh. In fact, you must encourage yourself to experience joy any time you can. It is vital to your survival.

Musician, writer, and activist **Antonio Michael Downing** also believes the stereotype of a "strong, unemotional male" is inherently problematic:

"When we talk about being a man ... 'Suck it up, power through, make it happen, be a man.' And what we mean by that is, 'Don't show any connection to your emotions because the standard is men think, women feel.' Which is, of course, nonsense because we're human beings and we all do both. What happens to the young boy [who is taught this stereotype] is he's cut off from his emotional toolkit, which is what he needs to process the craziness of this life. You need to be able to process emotion, to deal with emotion, to accept things, to process things. And so right at the time when you're feeling the most, the things you need to process, they get taken away."

Stephan Hawkins, the owner of Good Brotha's Book Café, agrees with Antonio:

"In the Black community, we tell our sons, 'Don't cry. Be a man. That didn't hurt. Get up.' I find myself doing that at times, but in general I teach my sons, it's okay to cry; it's okay to feel emotions. I believe Black men should be allowed to communicate how they're feeling, but here comes the warning: don't allow how you're feeling to dictate how you interact with other people. If someone made you feel bad, it doesn't

mean somebody else deserves that energy. Take the time to reflect on your feelings and address the root cause. You may be mad, but what is the root cause of this anger? Is it embarrassment? Is it annoyance? Is a frustration for real? Is it sadness? Did something happen to you when you were five, and now you're lashing out because you never properly dealt with the consequences? Sometimes, your first reaction is to give somebody anger and hate, when really, you're mad at somebody from 2001. Sometimes, you might want to confront the person who hurt you. Don't feel less of a man for saying, 'Hey, you hurt me, and this is how I'm feeling right now, and I don't want to feel like this.' Ignore those who call it acting real soft. Don't mind them. Yeah, we often have to put on a macho exterior, but you're allowed to be soft and vulnerable when the timing is right."

INTROSPECTION:

Make a Decision

Weighing decisions for very long takes up your attention and postpones the inevitable. Make a decision you have been weighing today. Look over your list of pros and cons, and then go with your gut. Knowing you have made a decision will teach you lessons in decision-making and make you feel more responsible.

Developing confidence in decision-making, through explicit decision-making practice, helps to reduce stress: When instances arise that call for decisions to be made, you will feel capable and confident in doing so, which will make you more resilient.

WEEKS 31–32: SPEAK UP, BE YOURSELF, AND GET OUT OF YOUR COMFORT ZONE

Be your own biggest supporter. Advocate for the things you want in all areas of your life. If you struggle with shyness, that can be hard, but there's no real reason to be shy. You'll face situations in your life that will require you to be more outgoing and to stand up for yourself. It's important that you learn to stick up for yourself when you need to because you won't always have someone there to protect your best interests. No one can make things happen for you but you, so speak up!

1. Collect your thoughts. When you are faced with a difficult situation, think about the issue at hand and take some time to collect your thoughts before responding. Share your thoughts and feelings in a meaningful way when you have an issue or feel uncomfortable. Don't hold it in because that won't solve anything. It will only lead to more discomfort and distress.

2. Value your needs. Know that your needs are important in both your professional and personal life. Do what makes you happy regardless of the judgment from others. Only you can live your life, so live it happily.

3. Own you. No one can be uniquely you in this world, so take up space and make yourself known. Always try to be the best version of yourself, no matter what. You deserve to be right here in this moment.

4. Get out of your comfort zone. Putting yourself out there and pushing your boundaries can lead to the greatest growth. You will find out that you are capable of so much more than what you or anyone thinks is possible. When you put your mind and determination to accomplish something, nearly anything is possible. Allow yourself to feel some discomfort

in this process. Growth can be uncomfortable, but you'll find that as you stretch yourself in new directions it will become easier to do.

- Push your comfort zone at school. Voice your ideas or criticisms. Ask for that one position that became open on the editorial board or student council. Pushing your own boundaries will help you to grow in confidence and learn about your own capabilities.

- Try a new activity. Maybe you want to try a dance class or an exercise camp. Challenge yourself with something fun. This can be a good opportunity to spark creativity and recharge.

- Have tough conversations. For example, if a friend says something that is inappropriate to a hurtful degree regarding race, sexual identity, or culture, tell them why you think it is wrong. Don't allow stereotypical language or behavior to go unchecked. Whether inappropriate or insensitive, call it out for what it is.

- Become more outspoken. It's important to be vocal about your values and what you want for yourself. When you don't speak up and make your opinions or feelings known, you lose out on an opportunity for respect and for your own happiness. Say out loud how you feel about an activity or an idea, and let others know when you are uncomfortable with those ventures or when you are excited about them. Be your own best friend and advocate.

Stand-up comedian **Hennessy Williams III** shares how he gets out of his comfort zone every day by being a stand-up comedian:

"I went the route [of stand-up comedy] and I decided to go on stage and just brave the unknown. The hardest thing about it? You really don't know how well you'll do that night. You don't know if [the audience] will like the material. But you have to get over that fear [before a show], that natural anxiety. I've learned from a bunch of comedians who say, 'You should never lose that small amount of nervousness, because if you do, then that means you're not doing stand-up the way you used to anymore. And now you're just kind of phoning it in.' "

INTROSPECTION:

Speak Clearly and Slowly

More assertive people speak clearly and slowly and say what's on their mind. Practice speaking clearly and slowly. Don't lift your voice at the end of a sentence as though you are asking a question. Watch your inflection and tone. Practice by speaking to a stranger every day, even if it is just to say hello.

Carefully choose your words to discourage negotiation and push back at times; this will allow for a more confident style of communication. When you communicate in ways that let others know something is not up for debate or that you know what you want and are doing, that contributes to your confidence and aids you when, in other instances, you're faced with communication that potentially challenges your confidence.

INTROSPECTION:
Mister CEO

Imagine yourself as the CEO of a company of your choice, perhaps one you see yourself running. Or imagine yourself as the invited motivational speaker come to address an audience in need of your knowledge, no matter what that is. Write that speech to yourself, but more importantly, look in the mirror and practice that speech. Record it on video and continue practicing to improve it.

WEEKS 33–34: BUILD MEANINGFUL CONNECTIONS

A part of creating a life you love is finding meaningful connections over a lifetime. You'll find people you click with instantly and people who will have your back during times of crisis. This could be your friends at school, a fraternity or organization you've joined to help build your confidence, or a coach or teammates on a sports club you've recently joined. You could also think about your church, your spiritual center where you rub shoulders with your peers or your pastors. Or maybe it's your family, your younger cousins or relatives who look to you for guidance, or your elders who like spending time with you, speaking and sharing ideas. These people are worth making an investment of time and energy because you will benefit from knowing them. These connections create fond memories and lessons learned.

1. Meaningful connections with friends and family help give support during tough times. Having a good support system is important for when you are going through tough times and need someone to lean on. This lets us know we are not alone and can talk about experiences in a safe space. Let your friends and family know they are important to you and that you appreciate them.

2. Choosing friends that spread happiness makes a difference for your mood. The energy you and others emit can be contagious, whether it is good or bad energy. It is very easy for us to match what we receive unless we decide to remove it. If you notice yourself feeling drained by someone's presence, ask yourself if the relationship is worth the trouble of maintaining. If someone is constantly pushing your triggers or upsetting you, it might be time to let them go.

3. Our sense of belonging is stronger when we build up the relationships around us. It is important to have a good support system and loved ones to help uplift us.

4. Focus on the present and on making happy memories. Focusing too much on the past or what will happen in the future can steal the joy from today if we let it. Make sure you are fully present when you are with friends and family. Put aside any distractions (like your phone) and be present in the moment.

5. Put in the effort to maintain friendships and relationships. Reach out to a friend or family member you have not spoken to or seen in quite some time. Let them know you are thinking about them and that you miss them. Nurture and build relationships you care about, and you will find more moments of happiness.

6. Share your life with positive people. Speak love and positivity to those in your life but also have friends who choose to do the same in your life. Uplifting each other can help us all grow in different areas of our lives.

7. Pet ownership is also a way to establish meaningful connections. Consider getting a cat or dog. Living with a cat or dog can be a wonderful thing. These pets can be there for emotional support and bring happiness to the home instead of fear or discomfort. They greet you when you come home, and the bonds we create with these animals can ease loneliness.

Here are several reasons why you should give pet ownership a try:

1. Improved mental health. Having a companion in your home can help with so many mental health issues. Dogs, for example, are known for their loyalty and unconditional love, and what's great about them is that they make you feel loved even when you don't feel this from your peers. They will join you on the couch when you have a mental breakdown, they cuddle with you, they lay their head on your lap when they sense your sadness, and they always have your back with companionship when you need to feel alive. We can learn and grow through the love of our pets.

2. Emotional support and availability. If you ever need to get something off your chest, you can vent to your pets. They can provide comfort without sharing a differing opinion and can be great listeners. Sometimes venting is just what we need to feel better and rid ourselves of the weight of that negative energy.

3. Positive hormonal impact. If you have a love for animals, you cannot help but become happier when around them. They are cute and huggable. Interacting with a pet, like cuddling and stroking them, has been shown to effectively increase feel-good hormones in both pet and human, and the bond that is formed between owner and pet is similar to a parent-child relationship. Stress relief is important for our health and having a pet you love can be perfect for this.

4. Companionship. A pet can give unconditional love to those who care for them. You can come home from a very hard day and the love of your pet can relieve any stress, anxiety,

or depression. Spend a little time cuddling your furry friend and see how a little love helps you feel less sadness.

5. Exercise. Go for walks with your dog. If you have an opportunity to practice yoga, you can get your dog, cat, and even your goat involved! This will get both of you moving, which is good for your mental and physical health. Fresh air and sunlight have a rejuvenating impact on the body and mind.

6. Playful engagement as a welcome distraction. Playing with your pet after a stressful day can be a good distraction from any frustration you may have encountered throughout the day. We all need a little fun away from all the stressors, so a game of fetch or playing with your pet's favorite toy can be a source of joy for you both.

If you can't get a dog or a cat, see if you can get a pet of another kind, like a hamster, turtle, or fish. If you can't get any kind of pet, try parenting a plant. They may not cuddle with you, but there is a movement nowadays to get Black people tending to plants, and it may have beneficial effects on your stress level. The point is to nurture something.

Matthew Kirby, the brainchild and creator of both Honest Human Resources Consulting LLC and *YNG BLK HR* podcast, believes in the importance of building meaningful connections:

"For me, my best practice is that you want to find your tribe. You want to find your inner circle. That could be a friend, best friend, a spouse, someone you like, someone who you can be vulnerable with. For me, when I think about my emotions, when times get really tough, I lean into vulnerability as a strength. I'm one of those people who says, 'Hey, it is always better to get it out versus keep it in.' "

INTROSPECTION:

Have a
Confidence Buddy

Find someone you really trust that you can rely on to boost your confidence when you are in times of need and do the same for them. You can have more than one confidence buddy, but make sure they are someone you can rely on to boost your mood. These relationships can add depth and perspective to your self-awareness: A confidence buddy can be reassuring when self-doubt creeps in and can also provide perspective and help with confidence blind-spots when/if you are having trouble channeling positivity and encouragement yourself.

WEEKS 35–36:
HAVE AN OPEN MIND

Creating meaningful connections requires you to have an open mind. This week, we will explore ways we can have an open mind and change our perspective. How can we change the way we approach life situations, whether personal or professional? How can we use perspective to help ourselves and others?

There are so many ways we can practice habits to change our perspective for the better.

Here are some ways to keep an open mind during the upcoming week.

1. Speak with people who may not view things in the same way as you. Having a friendly debate with someone is a great way to broaden your perspective on any subject. This is a wonderful way to practice having an open mind because you must be willing to listen deeply and formulate your own response. Sometimes you may not have the right answer, and in the process, your view may change. For example, have a friendly debate on the validity of pineapple as a pizza topping.

2. Try to understand the perspective of the other person when you encounter a disagreement. How do they feel about the situation? What might their experience be? How might their experience differ from your own? Asking yourself these questions will give you a better understanding of the situation and help you to resolve it.

3. Be open to the opinions of others. You cannot continue to learn if you are not open to hearing and learning from others' experiences and knowledge. This can also strengthen your relationship with people in your life by

offering an open line of communication between yourself and others. The world is filled with different people from different cultures and religions. You may meet someone who views social exchanges differently, and it's in these moments you should strive for understanding.

4. Sit down and listen to others' perspectives without interrupting. Really listen and take in what the other person is saying. This helps create a deeper understanding of the subject at hand. You will also be able to formulate a better-informed opinion, which will help when making important decisions. A friend may come to you with a personal issue and not necessarily want advice but just someone to hear them and sympathize with their feelings.

5. Try to view things on the side of gratitude. What good can come from a negative experience? What is the learned lesson? Oftentimes, when we are living with gratitude as our attitude, it allows us to open ourselves to a different perspective we didn't see before due to anger or frustration. The perfect time to practice gratitude is after a disappointing moment, such as not getting the acknowledgment you feel you deserve. Practice gratitude this week and try to form this as a good habit. This echoes our previous discussion on Weeks 25–26 about developing an attitude of gratitude, and it bears repeating because gratitude instantly grounds us and helps us remain connected to our sense of purpose.

6. Participate in activities or events that may be out of your comfort zone. The only way we continue to learn and grow is by challenging ourselves. This also connects to our previous mention of the importance of speaking up, being

yourself, and getting out of your comfort zone (see Weeks 31–32). You will learn more about what you can do through these challenging experiences, whether big or small. You can speak out during a class, share your ideas, or test your strength through a rock-climbing exercise. The smallest challenge can reap the greatest benefits.

7. Pause when reacting with anger. Anger can be a big deterrent to being a listener and to remaining open to any discussion at hand. When anger is the first reaction you have, take a pause and ask yourself why you are angry. This can easily be applied to arguments within a relationship. You may say something in the moment you later regret, and know you do not mean, but words hurt. To prevent unneeded pain, we should pause and think, "What about the situation has caused this reaction?"

Dealing with anger and frustration is even trickier when you are a Black man in the United States, when your own country uses media and narratives to constantly paint you as hostile and violent. Sometimes, a slight inflection in our tone of voice projects the wrong idea that we are flying off the handle, and it always falls onto us to maintain the peace. While this is difficult at times to navigate, remember that building confidence in yourself and finding joy are key, which means that we must keep our actions and behavior in mind. And while we cannot control the reaction of others, we can control our own attitudes toward maintaining mutual understanding and peace.

This, of course, is not encouragement for passivity. There are always moments in which debates become heated, or moments when it becomes clear that the person you engage with may not be valuing you as a human being. There may even be moments when they antagonize you on purpose or take away from your joy strictly to remind you to "stay in your place." Whatever the circumstance may be, it is imperative to retain dignity, your sanity, and your joy. Constantly debating people like this is exhausting and exploitative on their part. Mindfulness is key in helping you stay centered and reminding you of who you are and what the possibilities are if you choose not to engage in these debates. Protect your well-being at all times.

This also connects to our discussions about the constant practice of mindfulness.

Take the time to put these seven tips into practice this week to find which ones work for you.

Always remember that making important changes may take time, and do not be hard on yourself if you fall back into old habits.

Justin Black, author of *Redefining Normal*, struggled understanding why he ended up in the foster care system. Why did his mother leave him? Showing empathy—even when it seems nearly impossible given the circumstances—helped him deal with the trauma of his past:

"When I was a child and a teenager, I asked myself, 'Why me, why me, why me?' But when my mother surrendered us into the foster care system, she was just trying to do her best to support us and be the best parent she could be. She was a functional addict and she thought, 'This is the least amount of damage I can do,' if that makes sense. Understanding things from her perspective allowed me to work on forgiveness. I've learned to be more accepting of her, but also intentional about not letting that trauma pass down to the next generation, pass down to my children. I must be as intentional as possible about creating a safe space and environment for my children and children's children."

As hard as his experience was when he was young, Justin's experience reminds us that open-mindedness is helpful in building a better you. As we've previously discussed, this is a way of changing the negative into a positive outcome. By seeing his mother's intentions behind the hardship her actions created, Justin was able to be more accepting, to acknowledge his trauma but to also use this as a learning opportunity in order to not duplicate this reality for his own children. This is also a good opportunity to develop constant mindfulness in your life and find opportunities and mentorship to navigate those feelings. It may not be easy, but it isn't impossible.

"The hardest thing for a man to do is deal with himself, to introspectively confront his own emotional pain and trauma—so he can stop unjustly inflicting it on others."

—**Jason Wilson**, author, speaker, CEO of Yunion

INTROSPECTION:

Offer Suggestions When Making Group Decisions

When you are in groups of people who are trying to make decisions, speak up and offer suggestions. "We could go to the movies tonight to see..." is an example of how you can easily assert yourself. Don't allow yourself to be intimidated by a large group of people. Remember the others in the group might like to hear what you have to say.

Sometimes, asserting yourself means standing up to peer pressure, and these situations are not always comfortable. If your friends want to party and are engaging in underage drinking, or passing along smoking paraphernalia, they often expect you to follow suit. Asserting yourself means you will have to think of your own values and demanding they respect your wishes. This means having to say no. "I'm not into that," or "I'm going to sit this one out, thanks." It may be difficult, but you asserting yourself means you are treating yourself with respect and expecting they do the same. This connects to Weeks 31–32 when we discussed speaking up, and it will apply to other scenarios in your life, and even in your career when your future employers or coworkers expect you to jump at any time without respect for your boundaries.

WEEKS 37–38:
HOLD YOURSELF
ACCOUNTABLE

Holding yourself accountable is important to personal growth and mental health. Accountability means standing behind your commitments and following through on promises made. Personal accountability keeps us striving toward our goals and motivates us to do better. This week, see what you can do to make yourself accountable to your commitments.

1. Keep a schedule for yourself and make constant reminders. Put reminders with sticky notes around the house, on your phone, or in another place where you're sure to be reminded. Make reminders to remember social engagements and meetings.

2. Learn not to hold onto guilt but instead to learn and grow. Of course, that's easier said than done, because guilt is such a human emotion that is hard to let go. Here are some tools on how to dissipate guilt: In addition to mindfulness practice we have previously discussed, we are specifically thinking about how life isn't always black and white. There are gray areas when it comes to your actions, and you should instead focus on the in-between and break down in your journal the reasons why you feel guilty.

   Acknowledge to yourself that you are now in the present and that nothing can be done at this point to change what happened. Also, acknowledge that you are human, and that what counts is what you can do moving forward.

   Perhaps the most important tool you can use in cases like this is "self-forgiveness." This refers back to our discussion about practicing kindness and compassion toward yourself. Dwelling in feelings of guilt over things that we cannot change is detrimental. Guilt is a draining emotion, and it will have a powerful hold on you if you cannot learn to let go. Working through guilt can be a tough learning experience, but through the practice of self-love and self-forgiveness, you can eventually show yourself grace and mercy, and move forward with a growth mindset.

Guilt is a negative emotion that can make us less confident in our daily lives. Let's take guilt and turn it into a positive by asking ourselves why we feel guilty. Once you have found the answer, you can make a change for the better.

3. Let go of any negative emotions. It may not happen instantly, but we can work daily on our feelings and why we feel the way we do. Once we can understand why we have been so hurt or angered, we can try and move forward. Grudges only hold us back from joy.

4. Be honest. Accountability requires us to be honest with ourselves. We must be able to look at ourselves for our faults and skills to know how to be at our best. Does this sound familiar? Maybe it is because it again connects to self-love and showing yourself kindness. Part of that practice entails honesty, recognizing where we have made tough decisions and where we have made mistakes. It's okay to do so, even when it gets awfully uncomfortable. It is better to embrace that honesty and come out a better man for it—polished, more aware, more grown. One cannot become a diamond without having been put through the pressure and heat of the process.

5. Let go of imposter syndrome. This is a common experience among young people who feel driven to achieve greatness, even as they are on the way to that greatness themselves. You know that feeling you have of not belonging, or not being worthy in a group of people whom you consider

"achieved?" That feeling of not being good enough to get to that goal? This is very much connected to comparing yourself to others, as we have mentioned before. Stop telling yourself you're not good enough or that you can't do it and start speaking positive affirmations. Make your dreams your focus and work to make them a reality. Know that making mistakes is part of learning and doesn't mean you don't belong where you are; give yourself grace when learning from your mistakes.

6. Have a friend who holds you accountable and vice versa. An accountability partner can be helpful for a personal goal, such as working out or a career objective like getting a promotion. Having a friend to share your goals with can help to keep you motivated when you start losing steam.

SPOTLIGHT ON A BLACK ROLE MODEL

Writer **Geoffrey Philp** explains what accountability means for him:

"A gentleman has a code of conduct and something he holds himself responsible to, accountable to: his family, his friends, his country [...] [Martin Garvey] talked about self-reliance, and that is the essence of being responsible. I mean, that was one of the reasons why I left Jamaica. I knew I could never be a self-reliant writer in Jamaica. There were just no opportunities. I wanted to be self-reliant: I wanted to pay my rent on time."

INTROSPECTION:
Fake It Till You Make It

Try pretending you feel self-confident even when you don't. Step with a little more pep. Put on your favorite shirt and trick yourself into feeling more confident, even if it's just temporary. Sometimes confidence doesn't always feel natural when you're learning and practicing it but allowing yourself to embody confidence even when it feels unfamiliar is the best way to allow it to become more familiar. Practice over time will lead to it becoming more natural as time progresses. It also helps to know that many people who have achieved their goals, celebrities included, have practiced this to overcome their imposter syndrome. It helps to dress for the job you want as daily practice because it helps you "fake" the fact that you have made it. It creates that sensation in your mind that you know what you're doing, and you do. Many influencers who look like they're successful are creating an illusion for others on social media, but they're also creating that illusion for themselves so that they believe in themselves. Test drive that car and take pictures in it, practice that confidence in the new suit you bought, try that sockless look with your slacks and loafers, and step into social gatherings with a smile on your face to capture that feeling of confidence and smarts that you know you have but must practice.

WEEKS 39–40: DEVELOP HEALTHY HABITS

Movement can be good to release unwanted negative energies and stress and to bring happiness. Getting your body moving doesn't always have to consist of spending time in the gym. It can be any activity that pays homage to the body, recognizes its strengths and its work, and honors it with care. After all, our body is our temple; it is a dwelling, and the more attention you give it, the more it supports and carries you through life. There are so many ways to add healthy activities to your daily routine.

1. Eat healthy. Even if it means you have to eat vegetables regularly. Learn about what your body needs to fuel itself by studying nutrition, so you know which nutrients, vitamins, and minerals your body needs. Taking care of yourself shows that you care about yourself. This, in turn, makes you feel better about yourself. You'll also feel better physically and have more energy.

2. Move your body! Exercise can be a great way to get us moving during the week and can help with mental health. You might be thinking, "I hate exercise," but exercise doesn't have to be boring. There are so many physical activities to choose from—you just need to find the one that fits your taste and lifestyle. You may not be the type to like the gym, but hiking or biking are also ways to get out and move. What also helps is having a partner, someone who can help you stay motivated if you're going out rafting or tackling a 5K on a Saturday morning. Accountability partners are great because even if they're not doing the same sport or activity, they can still check in on you with a simple text message asking you to report your stats for the day. Exercise more. You'll feel stronger as a result, and you'll boost your body's endorphins—the "happy hormones" that make you feel on top of the world.

3. Appreciate your body. Another way to take care of your body is to show it some love. Stop tearing yourself down over a perceived flaw and speak positivity into your body. Your body carries you forward every day. The body is amazing, so let's give it some appreciation. Give yourself a massage and get comfortable with your body. Touch is a great way to show our bodies love. Self-massage can be a self-care ritual in and of itself. Close your eyes and rub the aches and soreness away from the muscles in your arms and back. Connect with your mind, body, and spirit.

4. Rest your body. You will know what your body needs when it needs it, if you are in tune to listen. When we are rundown from schoolwork or just life in general, we can have physical symptoms such as body aches, headaches, or overall fatigue. Listen to your body and rest. It is imperative to your overall well-being. Sleep is very important to our focus during the day and to our bodies' healing capabilities and overall health. Getting a good night's rest helps us to have the energy we need throughout the day. Having eight hours of sleep will help your body and mind to function at its best. When we don't get enough sleep, it can really impact concentration, critical thinking, and reflexes, among other things. Find ways to relax an hour before your bedtime. Read a book or listen to soothing sounds. ASMR (Autonomous Sensory Meridian Response) has become popular, but whatever you do, make sure it's free of screen time—no staring at your phone at 1 in the morning. You will notice improvement in your mood in the mornings once you get into the routine of getting the proper amount of sleep. Ensuring that we have enough sleep each night can also improve mental health for those who suffer from depression, anxiety, and more. It can cause you to be less

angry or irritated. Getting enough sleep prevents us from having a shorter fuse each day and helps us to have better social interactions.

5. Eat with mood in mind. Eat well. Our bodies do so much for us so let's give them some TLC. In addition, what we eat can influence our mood and vice versa. The food we give our bodies can really reflect in the way we feel. If we eat a lot of fatty foods full of sugar, this can cause heart problems and diabetes.

Eat a regular, nutritious breakfast every day. It is the first meal of the day, and it can really set the tone for your day. Eating a healthy breakfast will provide your body with energy, help brain function, and can still be yummy, too.

Do not drink too much caffeine. Caffeine can dehydrate the body and cause unwanted anxiety in some people. You may also find it hard to focus when caffeine has been overconsumed. Consider drinking decaffeinated coffee and tea if you must drink either coffee or tea.

Have a routine eating schedule. Stay hydrated and drink water throughout the day. Our bodies need to be sufficiently hydrated. Since our bodies are made up of around 60 percent water, it makes sense that dehydration will have us feeling tired and dizzy and experiencing headaches and other symptoms. Water is integral to all forms of life, so drink up!

Do not feel the need to restrict yourself but eat foods in moderation. Diets can become a bad habit, and anything consumed in excess can be bad for you. If you want to celebrate a promotion or a birthday, go right ahead. There is nothing wrong with having your cake and eating it, too. Just make sure it's only a slice.

6. Adopt a self-care ritual. Self-care can be the time of day you look forward to the most. It's your personal "me" time. Implementing a self-care ritual is great for mental health and overall well-being. It can help us to de-stress, clear our minds, and keep us creative. When we take care of ourselves, we nurture our potential.

    What does self-care look like for you? To answer this, you must really listen to what your body tells you it needs. Self-care is the time to realign the mind, body, and soul. It can take many forms, such as a meditation ritual in the evening, shooting hoops to decompress after a long day, committing to a weekly therapy session, or starting your day with yoga or reading. Do whatever gives you peace. Take a minimum of fifteen minutes a day for yourself. Always make sure you have a moment of respite, especially during a busy day. Give yourself time to close your eyes, breathe, and calm your mind. Take advantage of alone time. When you get the chance to give yourself alone time from family, school, or friends, make sure you take it. Time can get away so quickly, and before we know it, we are exhausted. Making the time necessary for any form of rest can prevent burnout.

    Take a bath instead of a quick shower. You can indulge in bath oils or exfoliants, or Epsom salt to soothe sore muscles if you've worked out or exerted yourself at work. Use beard oils and moisturize your hair, as a variety of products are now being made available for Black men to look and feel their best. Get a professional manicure or pedicure, or ask your barber for that fresh high fade you like. Cleaning your space can also be a form of self-care. Having a space that is decluttered and refreshed can help you feel the same. It can bring mental clarity, lift a mood, and bring overall happiness.

    Throughout this week, try to find your own self-care ritual that speaks to your personal needs. We all respond to different things in different ways, so you may try several things to find the perfect self-care ritual that works best for you. These self-care rituals may become acts you implement throughout your life.

7. Breathe and meditate. Practicing the simple meditation of focused breathing can be a great way to calm the mind and body. It shifts the mind from everything outside to within yourself, redirecting you back to yourself. For a few moments, you can try to forget outside worries and just breathe calmly. Try this exercise: Breathe in slowly through your nose for a count of seven, then exhale slowly through your mouth for a count of five. Repeat.

   There are different forms of meditation that have a positive effect on our lives. The key is to find the ones that bring calm and joy to you. You can Google different meditations to determine which ones work for you.

   Meditate with friends and share the moment. Sometimes just choosing to be a friend is a way to meditate. Maybe this person helps you to relax, laugh, and have fun.

   Bring goodness into the world around you when you are filled with love. Meditating and taking moments to take deep breaths, figuratively and literally, can open space within ourselves for self-love and happiness to spread love to others.

8. Keep social media and phone use to a minimum. Social media has a way of eating up time. You go on your phone to check one thing and, before you know it, you're in the black hole of social media. You can set up apps on your phone and computer to control how much time you spend on social media, but if you practice some discipline, you'll find it gets easier to step away from social media and focus more on what you need to get done. You can start by setting goals

to reduce the time you spend on social media by tracking your usage on your phone and setting alerts to let you know when you've reached your social media limit for the day.

If you're going to use your phone, do so to help manage your time. You can set up daily reminders to help you remember what you need to do next. There are apps that can help you with planning and organization. Working on tasks is easiest if you aren't distracted by people or social media. It might be a good idea to put your electronics away so you can focus on the task at hand. Some people find it beneficial to use time management techniques like the Pomodoro technique that suggests you work on a task for twenty-five minutes and then take a five-minute break, or the 52:17 rule where you work for 52 minutes then take a 17-minute break. You may find that breaking up the task into short increments of time helps you focus better.

If your work does not demand your phone be turned on, consider shutting it off. Sometimes, knowing the phone is lying there and is accessible to us can be a distraction. You can also choose to set an amount of screen time for yourself in the same way we do for kids. Some people even find it's easier to use a device as a reward for the work done that day, so checking our social media for five minutes after we have finished a project is a way to remain in touch without investing too much of our time in it. Even the blue light from your computer can become an issue if you consume too much of it as it disrupts your circadian rhythm. Consider shutting off all of this external stimulation about an hour before bed and disconnecting from these devices as much as possible to maintain a healthier you.

Limiting screen time and balancing your intake of external stimulations could be added to this list as well.

Andrew Bernard, owner of Make It Dairy-Free, practices a healthy lifestyle on the daily:

"I exercise at least five times a week, and it's healthy for me, not only physically, but mentally as well [...] My exercising, I do that for at least 30 minutes a day. It can be something as simple as just walking for 30 minutes, something like that, but I want to make sure I do something. I changed my lifestyle in terms of the way I eat, so I try to have more veggies, a lot more fruit, a lot less processed food. I stick to literally drinking water all the time. I drink nothing but water. And I want to say I get good rest often. I'm a strong believer in a good solid seven hours of sleep each night. So, even if my kids wake up before me, I try to get them back to bed with me. And then one more thing, I would say mentally, I'm always a student, so I try to keep my mind pretty sharp and keep myself aware and focused."

Dr. Uche Odiatu, coauthor of *The Miracle of Health*, combats the stereotype that real men don't do yoga:

"Yoga is all about flexibility and breath and breath work. It's not just about the pose and meditation and spiritual component to it. There are three modes of exercise: strength training, cardiovascular training, and flexibility training. Think of LeBron James in his late 30s or Tom Brady at 43. Any of these athletes

who are still playing their sport at 35 or 40 years of age, they do all three modes of exercise. 85 percent of the population don't do anything. The other 50 percent usually do one of them. Only 1 percent of the population exercises all three components. So, yoga is an easy way and a very structured way to give you the flexibility and balance portion. I think yoga gives you a really good foundation with breath work, flexibility work, and a consciousness to handle your day better. How is it not manly to be stable, conscious, and flexible? Everyone could benefit from yoga. [Yoga] is definitely something that a young man or teenage guy should try, and not think of as strictly something a woman might do. Yoga is for all people."

INTROSPECTION:

Listen to a High-Power Song

When you are feeling down, try playing a song that is high-powered. High-powered songs have a lot of bass and can improve your mood. Dance to the music while you're listening to it; stretch all your muscles and get your blood pumping. Music is a tool that allows us to pull ourselves out of a negative and unhealthy space. An upbeat song by our favorite artist/musician can lift our spirits and encourage movement that helps with tension in the body.

WEEKS 41–42: GO OUTSIDE!

Spending time outdoors is good for you. It helps you reconnect with nature and clears your head. You also get a boost of Vitamin D from the sunlight. Spend some time exercising outdoors, working in a garden, or just taking a walk. It will do you good.

1. Being outdoors can relieve stress. Immersing yourself in the sounds at a local park or hiking can have a calming effect. It's the opposite of the busy streets of daily life. Take some time this week to try it. Get out in nature, enjoy the quiet of the outdoors. Some find tremendous pleasure in exploring nature this way. In fact, the National Audubon Society recognizes Black Birders Week, during which African American bird watchers are invited to share their love of the outdoors and bird watching in hopes of boosting representation in the field of science and nature conservation. The outdoors benefits all of us, and spending time in nature is grounding and reinvigorating.

2. Uplift your mood and bring overall happiness. Going out by yourself can be another form of "me" time. Do something you enjoy such as hiking, shopping, or taking a brisk walk around your neighborhood. Offering your help to the elders in your neighborhood is a great way to feel like you contributed to others' happiness as well. Cooking them a meal or a simple pie and dropping it off unexpectedly is one of the best ways to create happiness. It might even help to offer getting their mail for them, or driving them to the post office, or getting them an extra batch of eggs on your next grocery run. Show up for your elders especially when they don't ask.

3.   Get inspired. There are so many different things to see out
     in nature or in the world—so many different sounds, colors,
     and textures. You will be amazed at the sparks of creativity
     that can be found. Spending a couple of hours at a museum
     or art gallery, connecting with your friends who are artists,
     or even listening to music can open you up to a sudden
     burst of inspiration for a project you didn't even know you
     had inside of you.

4.   Take yourself on a date. We don't always have to have
     another person to go on a date. Let's take ourselves out for
     once and treat ourselves like Kings. Sometimes it is easy to
     forget about taking care of ourselves and celebrating our
     lives. Simply going to a movie alone or grabbing a coffee
     and plopping yourself down in a comfortable chair at a tea
     shop with a good book are good ways to spend time with
     yourself. You can also go shopping for that pair of new
     sneakers you wanted, attend a book reading, or check out an
     art exhibit at the museum. You don't always need company
     to have fun. Taking yourself out on a date is a great way to
     explore your own thoughts and ideas and a great way for
     you to get to know yourself.

5.   Learn to be comfortable being on your own. Feeling
     comfortable to go out to the movies or dinner alone can
     bring so much confidence. Some people find it incredibly
     depressing to eat alone, yet it doesn't have to be that way.
     Many meditation teachers and Buddhist monks find joy
     and beauty in mindful eating or taking a stroll to practice
     meditative walking. Being on your own can often be a source
     of inspiration and an opportunity for spiritual growth,
     so enjoy it!

Getting outside by exercising, specifically, can make a world of difference. **Dr. Uche Odiatu**, coauthor of *The Miracle of Health*, explains why this is the case:

"Exercise, or any physical movement, changes how you breathe. Right away, you get an increase in endorphins. You have an increase in what's called encephalins and adrenaline, and your mind gets very expansive. And anytime you change the way you breathe, it changes how you think. So, if you're having a bad day and immediately you start running some stairs or you go for a walk, run, or go to a CrossFit class, immediately the brain thinks, 'Hey, you're breathing hard!' Endorphins are going, you have some dopamine going, and now it changes your mood. And then after you've finished, the world looks a little brighter. And maybe you're thinking, 'Dr. Uche, I hate exercise.' Well, after 30 minutes of changing how you breathe, it changes how you look at a situation. Because even now in Toronto, now it's a little after 7:00 or 7:30 p.m. here, and I've worked all day. But if I do a workout, when I get home, I will have energy for two or three more hours after."

This connects with our first discussion on Weeks 1–2 on building confidence, and on moving our body to develop healthier habits. Being indoors is one way to develop this, but being outdoors can help us connect with nature in a way we cannot do when we are inside, so we are improving a different level of our mental and emotional health while working out. Think of the outdoors as another gym where you can breathe in fresh air and feel connected to the world.

INTROSPECTION:

Do a Power Pose

Research has found that positioning your body in certain poses can help increase your self-confidence. Try one of these poses to see if holding the pose for two minutes helps:

- Stand with your legs spread apart, chest puffed out, both hands on your hips.
- Lean back in a chair with your hands folded behind your head and your feet up on a table.
- Stand up and lean over a table slightly with both hands on the table.
- Lean back in a chair with your hands folded behind you and one ankle resting on the other knee.
- Lean back in a chair with your legs separated and drape your arm over an armrest or chair next to you.

Just like a change of scenery and getting outside can do a lot for a person's mood and confidence, posing and putting our body in positions that make us feel powerful can do a lot to encourage us in times where we may feel an inclination to shrink or slouch when dismayed.

WEEKS 43–44:
MEMORIZE HAPPINESS
IN YOUR BODY

You carry memories in your mind of times and places you have experienced both joy and sadness. These memories are there for you to recall when you need a reminder of times past. This could mean memories of traumatic or harmful events experienced in your childhood, and your body recalls them as a way to keep you safe now, and to prevent you from repeating that experience. The body also carries intergenerational trauma, from experiences you may not remember in your immediate life, experiences inherited from your ancestors or community. This is what the study of epigenetics entails, understanding the effects that environment and behavior have on genes.

"Many of the times when trauma is thought to have echoed down the generations via epigenetics in humans are linked to the darkest moments in history. Wars, famines and genocides are all thought to have left an epigenetic mark on the descendants of those who suffered them."

—Martha Enriques, BBC.com, "Can the Legacy of Trauma be Passed Down the Generations"

You also carry memories in every cell of your body and can use them to recall pleasant times when you are down or upset. Those good memories may be ones from your childhood, time spent with your grandparents fishing or baking, moments when you've won athletic or spelling bee competitions, or evenings spent with your family playing board games and laughing wholeheartedly out of pure joy. Learn to memorize these moments and cultivate happiness so they can also enter your cells. You can do this using these tools:

1. Acknowledge positive emotions within your mind and body. When you are spending your time doing something you love, take the time to appreciate the happy emotions. We often linger on negative events and forget joy.

2. When in a negative space, practice recalling good emotions. Think about the times that brought you positive emotions and recall those times in moments of hardship. These hardships help us to appreciate the good in our life more and help lend us strength to endure, until the good comes again.

3. Use muscle memory. Our muscles have their own memory. When we exercise, when we draw or hike, our muscles develop a memory of the movements, even after we have stopped doing something for quite some time. Go back to something you love, such as painting, yoga, or anything that involves your muscle memory, and see how your ability to re-engage returns with ease.

4. Practice smiling. Smiling can be a simple way to lift your mood. Historically, men have urged women to smile more without realizing the need to smile themselves. It's time we help change this. Instead of expressing our need to boost our happiness through encouraging others to smile, we must plant the seeds for joy ourselves by practicing the art of smiling. The act of smiling can trigger a positive chemical reaction in the brain helping our mental health and reducing any stress.

    -   Smiling lifts the mood. Smiling tells our brains we are happy, even if we are not, and it can instantly ease us away from negative emotions. Maybe then, we can use coping mechanisms to process these emotions and transform that energy positively. Watching your favorite comedies is a way to not only smile and laugh, but it can also adjust your mood so that you step out of your house feeling more joyful. Funny memes and videos are also helpful in tickling our funny bone. It might also be helpful to spend time with your friends and relatives who always make you laugh, and you can also count on your pets. Playing with them are guaranteed to uplift your mood.

Smiling reduces stress. Just the act of smiling can help us come down from stressful moments. One way to do this is to allow yourself the joy of observing scenarios or films that make you happy or that are silly. Seeing children on a playground or a field can easily trigger happiness within. Observing their interactions with each other and their parents brings joy. You can even watch comedic movies to illicit a chuckle. You'll find yourself feeling more relaxed and more receptive just through laughter and smiles.

Smiling can help others smile. When you're walking down the street and a stranger greets you with a smile, how do you feel? Does it instantly bring lightness to you and make a smile come forth too? Try greeting strangers with a smile and see what happens. Even if you don't engage in conversation, it will help lighten the mood. You can also try this when receiving customer service. Even if the person helping you is in a bad mood, they will often at least relax and provide you with better service.

Smiling reinforces positive feelings. The body remembers we are happy when we smile, and it brings focus to joy rather than sadness. You can even try smiling at yourself in the mirror to stimulate those feelings of self-love and boost your own confidence. Although we have discussed minimizing your time on social media, you'd be surprised to find how taking a smiling selfie of yourself and sharing it with your close ones resets your mood but also that of others. Send a smile to someone you love who is ill, in the hospital, or who is feeling lonely. A smile can be a gift in itself, to yourself and to others.

When **Dr. Emmanuel Cherilien**, also known as Dr. Tank, gets in a bad mood or encounters a bad day, he takes a moment to reflect inwardly and realign his mind, body, and spirit so he can gain newfound perspective and move on:

"When I have bad days, I really get into a mental place where I penetrate inwards, and I just try to align myself and try to really remind myself what I'm here for, what I'm trying to do, and really just see what's going on internally. The other thing that I do physically is I go to the gym. Usually after I've finished my meditation and the physical, mental, and some would even argue spiritual parts, I tend to align myself back. I remind myself that there are bigger problems in the world, there are bigger things going on. The thing that I'm worrying about is probably minuscule compared to something else, so I just step back sometimes and say something like, 'Bro, take it easy. Life's not that serious.' And then for me, that helps me just align right back to what I need to do. So, I don't try to stay there long, but I just understand [bad days] are part of life. That's what I do. Physically, mentally, and spiritually take a step back and realign myself."

INTROSPECTION:

Smile

Even if you're not feeling it, smiling can be good for your heart rate and project an image of self-confidence. Try out these smiling exercises to increase your muscle strength in your face and give your confidence a boost:

- Stand in front of a mirror with your face relaxed.
- While keeping your mouth closed, stretch the sides of your lips as far as you can without showing your teeth. Hold this pose for ten seconds.
- Continue stretching your mouth until you expose the top half of your teeth. Hold this pose for ten seconds.
- Smile as wide as you can, showing all your teeth. Hold this pose for ten seconds.
- Next move through the exercise in reverse order starting with a teeth-baring exercise and moving to a closed mouth.
- Practice different ways of stretching your mouth. Open your mouth until your chin drops to your neck, place your fingers inside your lips and stretch them.

WEEKS 45–46: LET GO OF FEELING BUSY

Constantly feeling the need to do work or sharpening a skill can leave no room for rest or reflection. Trying to push ourselves to compete with others may also be detrimental to our own well-being.

Take this week to practice rest within your day and let go of the need to be constantly moving. See if adding a little rest time to your schedule helps keep you motivated and moving forward when you are on task.

This is important because of the stigma associated with Black people having to be twice as good or work twice as hard. We often feel we have to do more and go above and beyond to prove ourselves. Black people are constantly concerned about getting things right and achieving excellence, so that they are beyond reproach and so that they can justify their request for rewards they already deserve. Finding the right balance is key, and prioritizing yourself is key. This goes back to setting healthy boundaries for yourself. Black athletes, for example, spend much of their time defending their excellence under scrutiny, like Serena Williams having to undergo excessive doping screenings to make sure her excellence isn't due to cheating, or Simone Biles having to fight for her right to use her dangerous maneuvers during competitions. This can be toxic to you and overall, Black people have to realize that Black excellence and Black Girl Magic, as inspiring as they are in hashtag form, can be detrimental to our health. Don't take on too much, don't overwhelm yourself to prove a point.

1. Prioritize work/life balance. Structure your days for work and stop working when work stops. It can be very easy to let work take over your whole day. Some people may even take their work home after they leave the office. This can be an unhealthy habit that takes time away from other important aspects of your life.

2. Make sure not to run yourself down. Ensure that you leave yourself time to relax during the day. Take intermittent breaks throughout your day to prevent burnout. The act of taking breaks between things allows you to refocus and refresh to complete future tasks.

3. Streamline your tasks. Making your day flow more effectively and efficiently can make a big difference. Order and organization allow you to get more done in less time because you don't waste time thinking of what to do or scrambling for the necessary items to get things done. Planning and preparation are key components to streamlining your tasks.

4. Narrow down what is truly important. Look at everything you believe you need to do and really think about what is important right now. Once you determine what takes priority for you right now, do those tasks first. Organizing your tasks by level of importance and crossing them off as you complete them contributes to your sense of accomplishment.

5. Pace yourself based on yourself. Life is not a competition, do things at your own pace and timing. Do not overwhelm yourself with the perception that you must keep going based on the perception that you are behind or not doing enough.

Do you find that you are always busy with something? Hopefully, these tips are helpful and give you a little insight into the benefits of being less busy. You can still accomplish so much without the constant buzz around you.

Spend some time alone and do nothing.

1. We all need rest. Rest can be actual sleep or doing something to relax the mind and body. Rest allows us to slow down, heal, and feel refreshed to start anew. If we overwork ourselves, we slowly degrade the quality of our work, our joy, and our life.

2. Reset with alone time. Time alone can help us reset and see things more clearly. Taking the time to be in silence and reflect can be very important to our well-being. Introspection can help us think about things critically to make changes for the better. It can bring forth inspiration and a renewed excitement for things to come.

3. Do things that nourish and speak to your soul. You know the things that make you happiest and feel most fulfilled— do those things regularly. Incorporate these into your daily life, whether it is spending time with close friends or reading a novel.

Roderick Morrow, the host of the podcast *The Black Guy Who Tips*, recognizes the importance of balance:

"The podcast keeps me balanced. Because here's the thing: if you have a creative brain, it never takes time off. Even when the mikes are not on, my brain is still thinking of funny stuff, poignant stuff. I had to make a conscious decision to stop these thoughts. Podcasting has taught me to be careful and go, 'Hey, slow down.' "

INTROSPECTION:

Keep a
Confidence Journal

Journaling can help with resetting and taking time alone to reflect and process. Write down all the things you like about yourself in a confidence journal. Start your sentences with, "I'm great because..." Try this for fifteen minutes and see how many positive qualities you can find. Alternatively, find images in magazines that fit your best qualities and make a collage of them. Keep the collage or the journal where you can see it easily in times of need.

WEEKS 47–48:
CONSIDER THERAPY

There has always been a stigma on mental health and therapy, especially in the Black community where having issues with your mental health is considered a weakness. According to research from Columbia University's Department of Psychiatry published in 2019, "The Black community suffers from an increased rate of mental health concerns, including anxiety and depression. The increased incidence of psychological difficulties in the Black community is related to the lack of access to appropriate and culturally responsive mental health care, prejudice and racism inherent in the daily environment of Black individuals, and historical trauma enacted on the Black community by the medical field. Moreover, given that the Black community exists at the intersection of racism, classism, and health inequity, their mental health needs are often exacerbated and mostly unfulfilled."

Let's begin this week with an open mind and the knowledge that there is not only one way to apply therapy to your life. Take this week to explore therapy and find what works for you. If you are living at home with your parents, ask them if you can try a few sessions with a therapist. A good therapist can lead you to a better understanding of yourself and your lived experiences and best help you attend to your wants and needs. Black therapists are making themselves available and are out there openly wanting to help our community heal. This is essential because of the stigmas associated with Black people, mental health, and therapy, as well as issues regarding access to quality and affordable healthcare.

1. Rid yourself of the stigma against going to therapy. Getting help doesn't mean you are mentally incompetent. Therapy is a helpful source for getting an outside perspective to better understand the way you think and why you make the choices you do in your life.

2. Find the right therapist for you. You may go to your first session and not click with the therapist you chose. Do not be discouraged; keep looking until you find the right fit. You should feel comfortable sharing your feelings and experiences, not judged by the person you choose. You should make sure you leave your sessions feeling hopeful, like you can make progress.

3. Be open to help. You must go into this with an open mind and a willingness to seek help. Don't go because you feel outside pressure. Get into any form of therapy for yourself and because you want to progress on your personal journey in life.

4. Find the root cause. Therapy can help you determine the root cause for your stress, anxiety, or depression. It can also serve as an outlet for processing past experiences you may not have recognized have an impact on your present interactions and outcomes. Sometimes there may be direct reasons causing harm to our mental health, but other times, it can be a mix of different things coming from different areas in your life.

5. Find coping techniques. When you realize you cannot control your emotions, their intensity, duration, etc. therapy can help you find coping techniques or healthy ways to express your emotions. This could be simple journaling exercises that are guided by your therapist with mantras, breathing techniques to help you cope with anxiety, or a series of mantras or affirmations that you get into the mindset of repeating every day. There are also tapping techniques or other occupational therapy techniques to help you control your mind when your emotions spiral out of

control. Drawing on ancient Chinese acupuncture practices, tapping can be effective against stress and anxiety.

What are ways you acknowledge and learn from unhappy circumstances? Maybe share them with family and friends to start a conversation about growth.

SPOTLIGHT ON A BLACK ROLE MODEL

Zachary Nunn, founder of Living Corporate, encourages you to try therapy:

"I'm a big proponent of therapy. I have a therapist that I see at least every other week, if not every week. I think being transparent and being vulnerable with people, and creating a community, and having multiple resources to support you is important."

One-Minute Self-Esteem Exercise

Start this exercise by identifying an area in your life where you need to work on your confidence level. Some of us might need extra help with building that confidence, and it may take some therapeutic work to help you unblock the trauma that stands in your way. This is key to help you clean the energy around you and inside you, to help you build the self-esteem you need to move forward in life. Summarize why this area in your life is difficult for you. Then, write down the reasons you believe this area is difficult for you to work on. Next, identify the positive qualities you possess that will help you work on this area of your life. Ask a friend or family member to help you find positive qualities, if you have a hard time doing so. Lastly, ask yourself what lesson you are trying to teach yourself with this exercise. For example, "Even though I have a difficult time with algebra, I know if I study harder, I am smart enough to pass the class." Repeat this to yourself several times a day. Like Langston Hughes said, "I have discovered in life that there are ways of getting almost anywhere you want to go, if you really want to go." Determining what is difficult for you or what areas you need to work on is a good conversation to have in therapy, too, because a therapist can support you in making that improvement in your life.

WEEKS 49–50: TREAT YOURSELF LIKE A FRIEND

We have so much love and compassion for our friends, but sometimes we do not extend this love to ourselves. This week, you are going to challenge yourself to be more like a loving friend instead of your worst enemy.

1. Practice self-compassion. We often do not treat ourselves as kindly as we would our own friends. We may even treat a stranger with more kindness than we offer ourselves. Get into the habit of practicing compassion and apply it to yourself daily. When you have a bad day and do not perform at your best, do not tell yourself you are not worthy. Instead, encourage yourself that you can do better tomorrow. Don't let misgivings you have about yourself give you permission to berate your efforts.

2. Be a friend to yourself. Think about how you would treat a friend in comparison to how you treat yourself. Often, we will give a friend the benefit of the doubt, we will forgive, or we will lend a helping hand. Why do we not do these things for ourselves? Treating yourself like a best friend will help you change your relationship with yourself. You'll find you're putting yourself first more and looking out for your own best interests. You'll also feel more at peace with yourself, knowing you care about what happens to you.

3. Give yourself grace when you make a mistake. Change your thought process when it comes to your own mistakes. We all have our own faults and strengths, but you may sometimes focus more on your faults than your strengths. One way to approach a shift in mindset is to change a negative thought like, "It's all my fault" into one that offers grace, like "What can I do differently next time?"

4. Celebrate YOU. Every victory deserves a celebration because these small wins create the end goal. It is all a part of the journey, and when you look back on it, you will see how much you have accomplished.

- Focus on the parts of yourself you love. What about yourself makes you feel good and confident? Once you find the parts of yourself you adore, find ways to highlight them.

- Focus on what you have accomplished today. When it has been one of the most frustrating of days, it is easy to forget about how much work you have already done in moments of stress. However, thinking about your accomplishments can renew your confidence.

- Focus on your plans and goals. Getting excited about what we have planned can make our day ten times better. Take the steps you need to accomplish these goals, and watch your confidence grow as you achieve them.

- Reflect on your own personal journey. It is easy to overlook the work we put into our goals or not even realize when we have accomplished so much. This may be when you need to tap into your network of peers, be it friends or relatives, people who know you and can help you recall what you have overcome to get to where you are. It may also be a good time to revisit the journaling you've been doing. This is one of the best ways to take stock of the years that have passed, of your growth, of your journey, and you'd be surprised how much you have grown.

SPOTLIGHT ON A BLACK ROLE MODEL

Writer and filmmaker **Yanatha Desouvre** believes in the power of failing forward:

"I would tell my younger self to fail forward. It's okay to fail. It's okay to make mistakes. What's not okay is not learning from the mistakes. Figure out how can you grow from your mistakes. That's how your confidence will grow. I am a classically trained piano player. And when you play the piano, you're always asked to practice. I used to practice hours upon hours. Practice doesn't necessarily make perfect, but practice allows you to get closer and closer to where you want to be. I would encourage my younger self to set small goals—achievable milestones. But don't stop there. Build on those milestones. Take others with you that you trust and love, people who love you back and will celebrate your success with you. They will help you build your confidence."

INTROSPECTION:

Use a Mirror to Compliment Yourself

Stand in front of the mirror and compliment yourself. Smile and say nice things to yourself about your body, your intellect, your efforts. And when you see yourself in a mirror throughout the day, remind yourself of how awesome you are by talking to the mirror. Say, "What a handsome, smart man." In the same way that we often give compliments to our friends or in the way our friends compliment us, it's important for us to be comfortable in complimenting ourselves and in acknowledging and highlighting the good feelings we have about ourselves.

WEEKS 51–52:
BELIEVE IN YOUR
POWER TO
CHANGE YOUR LIFE

For any form of change to take place, you must first believe in yourself. Believe that you can make good changes. Those beliefs have influenced and led so many influential figures before us in heralding change. Congressman John Lewis and Dr. Martin Luther King Jr. set out to create change by making "good trouble." Contemporary athletes, like LeBron James and his I-Promise schools, and musicians like John Legend investing in educational programs, are examples of individuals motivated by the steadfast belief of creating change. Take these bits of advice into the week to give yourself the power to make the positive changes in your life.

1. Change what does not serve you. Without realizing it, we can sometimes become satisfied with the way things are going, even when they're not really going all that well. Take a moment to step back and look at the way your life has been unfolding. What about it does not serve your goals? What steps must you take to make things different? Once you do this, you can create meaningful changes.

2. Affirm yourself daily. Daily affirmations can be a way to build self-confidence in your life. Begin your days this week with positive thoughts. You can write down in a journal what you appreciate about yourself or what you want to bring into your day.

3. Overcome fear. Sometimes fear is the one step we must overcome to find happiness. Fear can be a big obstacle preventing us from accomplishing our wants and desires. Is your fear a fear of failure? Is it a fear of being weak or being judged for seeking help? It is okay to be vulnerable; you may even find strength in your vulnerability as you become more comfortable with it. Take the time to examine the root cause

of your fear and what you can do to transform that fear into positive drive.

4. Let go of negativity. Negativity comes in the form of energy, people, or situations in your life. Past regrets and negativity will only hold you back from the potential in your life. Someone may have had a tough upbringing with negative emotions toward their mom or have had an unfair amount of misfortune in their job, causing them to feel unworthy. It is okay to have a bad day, but a constant negative aura can prevent you from seeing the amazing possibilities in your daily life.

5. Choose your surroundings carefully. Choose to surround yourself with people who uplift each other. Surrounding yourself with good, loving energy can make the biggest change in how you move in your life. Leaning on your Black friends in times of need can be very grounding. Having shared or similar life experiences will ease anxiety and help you to know you are not alone. It will influence your mood daily and help improve your outlook on the situations you encounter.

6. Self-Reflect. Being introspective will keep us in tune to our own mind, body, and spirit. We can examine our mental state and physical health to learn to listen to what we need.

7. Set goals. Find out what your goals are for yourself. Once you can define what you want to bring into your own life, you can now start to work toward these goals.

8. Educate yourself! Value books, podcasts, and lectures. I'm suggesting the following role models for you to discover:

- Kenyatta Tucker-Ibarisha (he and his wife are behind Black Men Read, a community organization that fosters reading)

- Kwame Alexander, author

- Jason Reynolds, author

- Geoffrey Canada, educator

- Marc Lamont Hill, https://www.marclamonthill.com/about (he owns a bookstore now, too)

- Hill Harper, actor and author, among other things (he's great because he writes books about uplifting young Black men)

SPOTLIGHT ON A BLACK MALE ROLE MODEL

Speaking of changemakers, **Dr. Tank**, founder and leader of Tank EdDucates, LLC, effects change in his daily life by encouraging educators to better connect with and uplift people of color in their classrooms:

"So, I don't know if you're familiar with the school-to-prison pipeline, but that's a tag word we sometimes use while talking about what's happening in education. The issue is that Black boys are being funneled out of the school, and they're disproportionately expelled, suspended, and kicked out of school at a higher rate than their white peers. And what happens now, when you kick them out of school, they don't have the skills. They then go into the streets and then they often end up going to prison. So, what I try to do is dismantle that by teaching teachers, as well as superintendents and principals, how to connect with minority students. How do we diversify the curriculum, how do we include more Black history, change the textbooks, hire more teachers of color? And so, I believe by doing that, you're connecting better with their culture and their history. And therefore, their students will be engaged."

INTROSPECTION:
Face One Fear Everyday

Fear is like a butterfly in your stomach. You'll know you're facing a fear when you get that feeling of flightiness in your gut. So, the next time you feel this feeling, don't back away from it. Instead lean in and see what happens. Try to face at least one fear every day. Start with easy fears that are minor and work your way up to the big ones. This can be tricky because what is easy for us can be a massive hurdle for others. Let's say you are afraid of drowning: one easy step toward conquering that fear can be to dip your toes in the water just to start, and then hiring an instructor to help you gradually conquer that fear by learning to swim. A harder fear may be public speaking, which may call for you to step up in front of smaller crowds at first, just one or two friends and then gradually expanding to larger crowds in hopes of conquering that fear. Change is created slowly, especially when fear is involved. Eventually though, the little changes add up to big shifts in things. So, it's okay to be afraid of something, but it's important that you "do it scared" to overcome that fear and reach an accomplishment because often, growth is on the other side of our fear.

All the Very Best in Life!

Now that you've read this book and practiced the exercises, you should have a better relationship with yourself and have noticed some changes in how you feel. You should have a clearer understanding of what self-confidence is and why it's important to develop your self-esteem. If you haven't achieved that to the fullest yet, however, don't give up. Show yourself kindness and grace.

This book was designed for you to spend time dwelling on possibilities, to help you imagine what life could be for you once you're ready to tackle its challenges, to help you see the future and help prepare you for it. In other words, take your time with the book. If you're finding you need more time to reflect or implement tools this book gives you, if you need an extra day or two, that's alright. Sit with it as long as you need, there is no rush. Stepping out in confidence implies a certain level of understanding and trust with the material.

You can revisit any of the chapters in this book anytime you need a reminder of how capable you are of achieving great things. The role models are there for you to look up to. Revisit them as often as you'd like to find men who have developed the kind of self-confidence you need to succeed in life. This book is also something you can pass on to the ones coming after you as you build your legacy. If not your kids, your mentees, your cousins—anyone looking for a handbook on walking boldly. You can also use this book as reference whenever someone comes to you for advice, whether it is seeking help in setting their values or needing a tip or two on how to be more assertive. Knowing what you know now, nothing can stop you for guiding them. You can even share this book with them.

I wish you all the very best in life. I believe we create our own futures, and I can't wait to see what you put together for yourself. The future is so bright. Put your best foot forward and walk out boldly. You got this!

They Walk Boldly

Oluwatoyin Ayanfodun was born and raised in Brooklyn, New York. He founded Tomorrow's Leaders NYC in 2011 to help underserved youth in middle schools. He earned a degree in Elementary Education with a minor in Entrepreneurship from Temple University and has a certification in Nonprofit Management from Temple University. Oluwatoyin was named an Echoing Green Fellow in 2015. In the spirit of gratitude, he uses his time to give back by helping uplift middle school kids who have few resources and teaches them they have the power to change their lives.

Phillip Bacon, CEO/President of Urban Philanthropies, has over twenty years' experience in real estate and community development. As a small business consultant with the Minority Business Development Center, he advised and wrote a number of successful businesses plans for some of Broward County's leading businesses. He worked as an economic development representative at the City of Ft. Lauderdale were he eventually became the department manager. He served as the Northwest Community Redevelopment Agency Manager and Real Estate Project Manager at Ft. Lauderdale before departing to become executive director of the Overtown Civic Partnership at the Collins Center for Public Policy. Prior to leaving the Collins Center, Mr. Bacon was vice president of neighborhood and regional initiatives where his responsibilities included designing economic development initiatives for clients statewide. Mr. Bacon currently is the president of Urban Philanthropies which he describes as a "civic entrepreneur." "Our mission is to help develop entrepreneurship in dis-invested communities." Mr. Bacon thinks that Urban Philanthropies will be impactful in helping to build civic and economic infrastructure in local communities like Overtown in Miami.

Andrew Bernard, from Make It Dairy-Free, has a degree in Visual Arts. He and his wife, Larisha, started Make It Dairy-Free after Larisha had to be dairy-free while breastfeeding. The site is filled with vegan and plant-based recipes that are all dairy-free. Many Black people lack the gene needed to process dairy products, which makes it difficult for them to digest their food. Going dairy-free may not be necessary for you, but paying attention to your health is important, and nourishing your body is a great way to start.

Justin Black, author of *Redefining Normal*, lived in abandoned houses in the poorest section of Detroit before his parents surrendered him to CPS at the age of nine. He stayed in the child welfare system until he graduated from high school. His journey toward healing is an inspiring one.

Albert Campbell is an executive member of The Circle of Brotherhood, an organization of primarily Black men from all walks of life that advocates for improved economic development, crime prevention, educational services, and youth mentorship. A reformed convict, Albert uses prayer as a form of meditation.

Dr. Emmanuel Cherilien, also known as Dr. Tank, is the founder and leader of Tank EdDucates, LLC, a nonprofit organization dedicated to educating underserved populations in life skills. Dr. Tank holds a Doctorate of Education and has more than twenty years of experience in the fields of education and leadership. He currently serves on the Board of Directors for Catholic Partnership Schools. Dr. Tank is a certified motivational speaker and helps to dismantle the school-to-prison pipeline through his work. He is the director of T.A.N.K. Mentoring in twenty-one New Jersey counties, and through that role, he helps ex-prisoners reintegrate into society successfully. Dr. Tank is also a professor and education consultant.

He has experience in and knowledge of business administration, criminal justice, sociology, philosophy, and history. He is dedicated to uplifting youth and encouraging them to pursue higher education and embraces kindness and empathy in his own way.

Yanatha Desouvre is a writer and filmmaker who was born in Port-au-Prince, Haiti and grew up in Brooklyn, NY, and Philadelphia, PA. He received his bachelor's degree in Management Information Systems (MIS) and Marketing at Drexel University in 2001 and completed his MBA in Marketing and Mass Communication and Media Management at Lynn University in June 2010. Yanatha works full time on the faculty of Entrepreneurship at Miami Dade College. Yanatha is the author of *An Essential Guide to Windows 10*. He's a Marketing and Information Technology coach and consultant who has taught at Miami Dade College and Chestnut Hill College. His literary works include *Walk Through this Journey*, *A Family Affair*, *To Whom Much is Given*, *Savor the Moments*, *Proud to Be*, and his bestselling children's book *Big Sister, Little Sister*, which is available in French, Spanish, and Haitian Creole. As a poet and motivational speaker, he's participated in many events for Drexel University, Lynn University, Palm Beach Atlantic University Literary Café, The Stage, World Café Live in Saul Williams "Chorus" Spoken Word World Tour 2012, and WURD's Summer of Freedom Tour 2013. Yanatha celebrates his achievements and always sets goals for himself, raising the bar higher and higher.

Antonio Michael Downing grew up in southern Trinidad, Northern Ontario, Brooklyn, and Kitchener. He is a musician, writer, and activist based in Toronto. His 2010 debut novel, *Molasses* (Blaurock Press), was published to critical acclaim. In 2017, he was named by the RBC Taylor Prize as one of Canada's top Emerging Authors for nonfiction. He performs and composes music as John Orpheus.

Stefan Hawkins is the owner of Good Brotha's Book Café, the first Black-owned coffee and book shop in Harrisburg. "I wanted to show that representation matters because a lot of times our youth [don't] see themselves in books, they don't see themselves reflected in movies," Stefan said. "So, I wanted a space where kids could come and see books that look like them."

Matthew Kirby is the brainchild and creator of both Honest Human Resources Consulting LLC and *YNG BLK HR* podcast. Matthew is a native of Fayetteville, North Carolina. He was raised in a low-income, single parent home and went on to become the first to graduate in his family from both undergraduate and graduate schools. Matthew earned a Bachelor of Arts in Psychology with a Spanish minor at the North Carolina Agricultural and Technical State University. He went on to earn a Master of Arts in Industrial and Organizational Psychology at the Chicago School of Professional Psychology. Matthew started his career working in the shredding industry as a human resource assistant. There, he learned how to spot talent, how to manage employee relations, and about payroll and benefits. He has also worked in staffing, finance, IT/Tech, and in the nonprofit sector. Along the way, he developed expertise in his field. He now works in the San Francisco Bay area, where he manages more than thirty clients. Matthew's approach to human resources is much different than the typical. He hosts a weekly podcast called *YNG BLK HR* that is engaging and interesting. His podcast is geared toward both HR professionals and those not in the field. He teaches people how to know their self-worth is important when looking for a job and helps them find employment by teaching them resume and cover letter revision, how to prepare for interviews, job search assistance, and how to relocate for a job opportunity. Knowing your self-worth, according to Matthew, is the first step in expecting and demanding the best for yourself and setting yourself up for success.

Roderick Morrow and his wife, Karen, are a southern married Black couple who enjoy pop culture and comedy. Their podcast, *The Black Guy Who Tips*, has been mentioned in The Huffington Post, The Daily Beast, *The Washington Post*, *The New York Times*, *The Los Angeles Times*, Bloomberg.com, Vox.com, BET.com, and Ebony.com. The show has also been featured on National Public Radio, Revolt TV, and *Vice News Tonight* on HBO. They are now exclusively on Spotify but were the number one comedy podcast at Podmatic. They have had many notable guests on their show, such as NBA shooting guard Anthony Morrow and ESPN contributor Bomani Jones. They have also been part of several audio plays and were featured in the film *Dirt Cheap Therapy*. Rod knows to value people who work in the service industry, and he shows his value for them by tipping. It is important to look out for others who earn less wages, while making sound investments in your own savings and future.

Zachary Nunn has a background in human resources. He saw the need for Black and brown voices to be amplified and started Living Corporate, a media engine that offers web shows, a blog, podcasts, and other media focused on Black and brown people in the corporate world. Zach didn't build his media empire in one day. He started out with an idea and found ways to grow it into a blossoming business venture.

Akili Nzuri, the creator of the Instagram page *A Black Man Reading*, teaches high school English in Mississippi. He's also a PhD candidate in a higher education administration program at the University of Southern Mississippi. An aspiring writer, Akili is working on a novel and a poetry collection. He's a husband and a father who enjoys lifting weights, playing basketball, and spending time with his family. Above all else, he spends a lot of time reading.

Dr. Uche Odiatu is a Doctor of Dental Medicine (DMD). He is a professional member of the American College of Sports Medicine (ACSM), a Certified Personal Trainer through the National Strength and Conditioning Association (NSCA), and a member of the Canadian Association of Fitness Professionals (CanFitPro). He is also the coauthor of *The Miracle of Health* and has lectured in Canada, the USA, the Caribbean, the UK, and Europe. He's been an invited guest on over 400 TV and radio shows from ABC 20/20, Canada CTV AM, Breakfast TV to Magic Sunday Drum FM in Texas. On his website, www.druche.com, and on Instagram, Dr. Uche shows the importance of physical fitness and yoga and their benefit to helping the body/mind connection.

Jehiel Oliver is an entrepreneur and the founder and CEO of Hello Tractor. Hello Tractor connects tractor owners with farmers in need of tractor services. At Hello Tractor, Jehiel manages operations and finds strategies to make sure the company is running smoothly. He has received numerous awards and honors for his work, including being recognized by *Foreign Policy* magazine as a Top 100 Global Thinker for 2016. The Obama Administration appointed him to serve two years as a member of the President's Advisory Council on Doing Business in Africa. Before working at Hello Tractor, Jehiel worked as a consultant and investment banker. Jehiel saw a need for small farmers to connect with those who had tractors and built it into a business, even though he was already working in a field that paid well. His ability to pinpoint a specific need and build a business around it stems from his organizational skills, which he acquired with the discipline in setting goals through lists and calendars and maximizing his time. The less hours wasted on social media, the more time he found to center himself, to think, and to identify needs in his environment.

Marlon Peterson has written, created programming, lectured, organized, and advocated alongside the formerly incarcerated, victims of gun violence, womxn, immigrants, and young people. Marlon is the author of *Bird Uncaged: An Abolitionist's Freedom Song*, the host of the *DEcarcerated Podcast*, and the owner of his own social impact endeavor, The Precedential Group Social Enterprises, and its nonprofit arm, Be Precedential, Inc. His TEDtalk, "Am I not human? A call for criminal justice reform," has amassed over 1.2 million views.

Geoffrey Philp is a writer who was born in 1958 in Jamaica. He is the author of five books of poetry, two novels, two collections of short stories, and three children's books. He earned his Master of Arts at the University of Miami and has taught at Miami Dade College. Geoffrey's books deal with different aspects of Caribbean culture and Blackness, including what it's like to grow up fatherless, Caribbean religions like Rastafarianism, Christianity, and African folklore. He's earned many awards for his writing, including an Individual Artist Grant from the state of Florida, a James Michener fellowship from the University of Miami, and an artist in residency at the Seaside Institute. A recipient of the Luminary Award from the Consulate of Jamaica, Geoffrey's work is featured on The Poetry Rail at The Betsy, an homage to twelve writers that shaped Miami culture. Geoffrey knows when he sits down to write that he's got something important to say in his writing. As a result, he works hard at developing his work and sets goals for himself to keep himself accountable.

Tim Salau is the cofounder and Executive Creative Chairman of Guide, the collective that owns Big Black Tea, a direct-to-consumer tea brand, and their keystone product, Guide, a learning and talent development platform. Tim armed himself with patience and learned to enjoy the process to get to where he is today. He is an artist, author, venture investor, builder capitalist, accomplished international keynote speaker, and tech leader. In 2017, he founded The Guide Group, a global movement of more than 300,000 business leaders and professionals focused on helping every member lead a fulfilling career. He's been recognized by and works with clients such as Amazon, PTC, Google, Microsoft, LinkedIn, Forbes, Toptal, the *Wall Street Journal*, the Honduran government, Omani Ministry, the Young Presidents Organization, SXSW, and The Millennial Mogul. Prior to founding and leading Guide, he led product and innovation with four global Fortune 500 companies: Google, Microsoft, Facebook, and WeWork, coaching CEOs, executives, and government leaders on how they can transform their workforce.

Hennessy Williams III is a stand-up comedian. He was born in 1989. Hennessy is one of the fastest-growing comedians in stand-up today. He has worked alongside Russell Peters, George Wallace, and the cast of MTV's *Wildin' Out*. Hennessy brings an edge to his style of comedy because he's not afraid to say outrageous things to get a laugh, a technique he developed throughout his career by stepping out of his comfort zone and pushing the limits for himself and his audience.

About the Author

Born in Port-au-Prince, **M.J. Fievre,** BS Ed, is a long-time educator and writer. M.J. earned a bachelor's degree in education from Barry University. A seasoned K–12 teacher, she spent much time building up her students, helping them feel comfortable in their own skin, and affirming their identities. She has taught creative writing workshops to children at the O, Miami Poetry Festival and the Miami Art Museum, as well as in various schools in Santa Cruz de la Sierra (Bolivia), Port-au-Prince (Haiti), and South Florida. As the ReadCaribbean program coordinator for the prestigious Miami Book Fair, M.J. also directs and produces the children's cultural show *Taptap Krik? Krak!*

Mango Publishing, established in 2014, publishes an eclectic list of books by diverse authors—both new and established voices—on topics ranging from business, personal growth, women's empowerment, LGBTQ studies, health, and spirituality to history, popular culture, time management, decluttering, lifestyle, mental wellness, aging, and sustainable living. We were recently named 2019 *and* 2020's #1 fastest-growing independent publisher by *Publishers Weekly*. Our success is driven by our main goal, which is to publish high-quality books that will entertain readers as well as make a positive difference in their lives.

Our readers are our most important resource; we value your input, suggestions, and ideas. We'd love to hear from you—after all, we are publishing books for you!

Please stay in touch with us and follow us at:
Facebook: Mango Publishing
Twitter: @MangoPublishing
Instagram: @MangoPublishing
LinkedIn: Mango Publishing
Pinterest: Mango Publishing
Newsletter: mangopublishinggroup.com/newsletter

Join us on Mango's journey to reinvent publishing, one book at a time.

CPSIA information can be obtained
at www.ICGtesting.com
Printed in the USA
JSHW031656240522
26261JS00001B/4

9 781642 507331